Cambridge English

ADVANCED

2

WITH ANSWERS

AUTHENTIC EXAMINATION PAPERS

Cambridge University Press
www.cambridge.org/elt

Cambridge English Language Assessment
www.cambridgeenglish.org

Information on this title: www.cambridge.org/9781316504505

© Cambridge University Press and UCLES 2016

First published 2016

Printed in Spain by GraphyCems

A catalogue record for this publication is available from the British Library

ISBN 978-1-316-50450-5 Student's Book with answers
ISBN 978-1-316-50449-9 Student's Book with answers with Audio
ISBN 978-1-316-50447-5 Student's Book without answers
ISBN 978-1-316-50448-2 Audio CDs (2)

Contents

Introduction

This collection of four complete practice tests comprises papers from the *Cambridge English: Advanced (CAE)* examination; students can practise these tests on their own or with the help of a teacher.

The *Cambridge English: Advanced* examination is part of a suite of general English examinations produced by Cambridge English Language Assessment. This suite consists of five examinations that have similar characteristics but are designed for different levels of English language ability. Within the five levels, *Cambridge English: Advanced* is at Level C1 in the Council of Europe's *Common European Framework of Reference for Languages: Learning, teaching, assessment*.

It has been accredited by Ofqual, the statutory regulatory authority in England, at Level 2 in the National Qualifications Framework. The *Cambridge English: Advanced* examination is recognised by educational institutions, governmental departments and employers around the world as proof of the ability to follow an academic course of study in English at university level and communicate effectively at a managerial and professional level.

Examination	Council of Europe Framework Level	UK National Qualifications Framework Level
Cambridge English: Proficiency Certificate of Proficiency in English (CPE)	C2	3
Cambridge English: Advanced Certificate in Advanced English (CAE)	C1	2
Cambridge English: First First Certificate in English (FCE)	B2	1
Cambridge English: Preliminary Preliminary English Test (PET)	B1	Entry 3
Cambridge English: Key Key English Test (KET)	A2	Entry 2

Further information

The information contained in this practice book is designed to be an overview of the exam. For a full description of all of the above exams, including information about task types, testing focus and preparation, please see the relevant handbooks which can be obtained from Cambridge English Language Assessment at the address below or from the website at: www.cambridgeenglish.org

Cambridge English Language Assessment
1 Hills Road
Cambridge CB1 2EU
United Kingdom

Telephone: +44 1223 553997
Fax: +44 1223 553621
email: helpdesk@cambridgeenglish.org

The structure of *Cambridge English: Advanced* – an overview

The *Cambridge English: Advanced* examination consists of four papers.

Reading and Use of English   1 hour 30 minutes
This paper consists of **eight** parts, with 56 questions. For Parts 1 to 4, the test contains texts with accompanying grammar and vocabulary tasks, and separate items with a grammar and vocabulary focus. For Parts 5 to 8, the test contains a range of texts and accompanying reading comprehension tasks.

Writing   1 hour 30 minutes
This paper consists of **two** parts which carry equal marks. In Part 1, which is **compulsory**, candidates must write an essay with a discursive focus of between 220 and 260 words. The task requires candidates to write an essay based on two points given in the input text. They need to explain which of the two points is more important and give reasons for their choice.

In Part 2, there are **three** tasks from which candidates **choose one** to write about. The tasks include a letter, a proposal, a report and a review. Candidates write between 220 and 260 words in this part.

Listening   40 minutes (approximately)
This paper consists of **four** parts with 30 questions. Each part contains a recorded text or texts and corresponding comprehension tasks. Each part is heard twice.

Speaking   15 minutes
The Speaking test consists of **four** parts. The standard test format is two candidates and two examiners. One examiner acts as both interlocutor and assessor and manages the interaction either by asking questions or providing cues for the candidates. The other acts as assessor and does not join in the conversation. The test consists of short exchanges with the interlocutor and with the other candidate, an individual long turn, a collaborative task involving both candidates, and a discussion.

Grading

Candidates will receive a score on the Cambridge English Scale for each of the four skills and Use of English. The average of these five scores gives the candidate's overall Cambridge English Scale score for the exam. This determines what grade and CEFR level they achieve. All candidates receive a Statement of Results and candidates who pass the examination with Grade A, B or C also receive the *Certificate in Advanced English*. Candidates who achieve Grade A receive the *Certificate in Advanced English* stating that they demonstrated ability at Level C2. Candidates who achieve Grade B or C receive the *Certificate in Advanced English* stating that they demonstrated ability at Level C1. Candidates whose performance is below C1 level, but falls within Level B2, receive a *Cambridge English* certificate stating that they have demonstrated ability at Level B2. Candidates whose performance falls below Level B2 do not receive a certificate.

For further information on grading and results, go to the website (see page 5).

Test 5

READING AND USE OF ENGLISH (1 hour 30 minutes)

Part 1

For questions **1–8**, read the text below and decide which answer (**A, B, C** or **D**) best fits each gap.
There is an example at the beginning (**0**).
Mark your answers **on the separate answer sheet**.

Example:

0 A appreciated   **B** valued   **C** achieved   **D** created

0	A	B	C	D
	▭	▭	▬	▭

The Golden Gate Bridge

The Golden Gate Bridge in San Francisco **(0)** …….. worldwide fame almost immediately after its completion in 1937, not just because it was a technical masterpiece but also **(1)** …….. of its elegant design. The eye-catching orange-red colour of the bridge also **(2)** …….. its popularity.

Construction of the road bridge started in 1933. At the time, many people doubted whether it was technically possible to span the 1,600-metre-wide strait. But despite this, the project **(3)** …….. . There is also a sidewalk for pedestrians on the bridge but it's quite a **(4)** …….. to walk across it. For a start, it is three kilometres long and 67 metres above sea level. In extreme weather conditions, the bridge can **(5)** …….. almost eight metres, which can make the crossing rather unpleasant.

The Golden Gate Bridge is at its most **(6)** …….. in the morning when it is often shrouded by mist. At night, it's also spectacular because the lighting makes it seem as if the towers are **(7)** …….. into the darkness. The bridge has long since **(8)** …….. its record of being the longest bridge but it is still one of the world's most famous landmarks.

1	**A** in the event	**B** on behalf	**C** as a result	**D** with the aid
2	**A** boosted	**B** intensified	**C** developed	**D** amplified
3	**A** went ahead	**B** moved off	**C** started out	**D** sprang up
4	**A** hazard	**B** challenge	**C** trial	**D** difficulty
5	**A** shake	**B** bounce	**C** sway	**D** wobble
6	**A** desirable	**B** enchanting	**C** glowing	**D** pleasurable
7	**A** dispersing	**B** separating	**C** spreading	**D** disappearing
8	**A** thrown	**B** lost	**C** missed	**D** resigned

Part 2

For questions **9–16**, read the text below and think of the word which best fits each gap. Use only **one** word in each gap. There is an example at the beginning (**0**).

Write your answers **IN CAPITAL LETTERS on the separate answer sheet**.

Example: | 0 | W | H | E | N | | | | | | | | | | | | | |

Doodling Is Good

The next time you are caught doodling, that is making unconscious or unfocused drawings **(0)** .... you should be listening, declare that you are simply trying to boost your concentration. Recent research suggests that, **(9)** .... than something to be frowned on, doodling should be actively encouraged because it improves our ability to pay attention. A study which compared **(10)** .... well people remembered details of a dull speech found that people who doodled throughout retained much more information than those trying to concentrate on listening.

Doodling, however, is not the same as daydreaming. It is quite common **(11)** .... people to start daydreaming when they are stuck in a boring lecture **(12)** .... listening to a tedious discussion, and then to pay little attention to what is **(13)** .... on around them. But the research suggests that doodling should no **(14)** .... be considered an unnecessary distraction. Not **(15)** .... is doodling sufficient to stop daydreaming without affecting our task performance, it may actually help keep us **(16)** .... track with a boring task.

Part 3

For questions **17–24**, read the text below. Use the word given in capitals at the end of some of the lines to form a word that fits in the gap **in the same line**. There is an example at the beginning (**0**).

Write your answers **IN CAPITAL LETTERS on the separate answer sheet**.

Example:

0	S	A	L	T	Y													

Super Rice

Rice crops fail in drought conditions or where the soil is
too **(0)** .... So work is underway to 'climate-proof' rice   **SALT**
so it can grow in even the most **(17)** .... of conditions.   **FAVOUR**
Drought affects 23 million hectares of rice annually, and
salt is equally **(18)** .... ; it reduces yields by 40% and   **PROBLEM**
consequently **(19)** .... the pressures on food supplies. Further   **INTENSE**
reductions in yields are likely due to climate **(20)** ....   **STABLE**

Scientists are attempting to produce a super rice by mixing genes
from drought-tolerant plants with those from another that exploits
nitrogen **(21)** .... , thus enabling it to grow without fertiliser.   **EFFECT**
Comparing the new rice's **(22)** .... with that of ordinary rice, the   **PERFORM**
super rice produced 17% more than the ordinary variety in individual
trials and 42% more when subjected to a combination of stresses.
In addition, researchers are working on improving other crops.
For example, one team has developed a potato that is **(23)** ....   **RESIST**
to certain diseases. It is hoped that developments such as this will
(24) .... the impact of climate change in developing countries.   **LESS**

Part 4

For questions **25–30**, complete the second sentence so that it has a similar meaning to the first sentence, using the word given. **Do not change the word given.** You must use between **three** and **six** words, including the word given. Here is an example (**0**).

Example:

0 James would only speak to the head of department alone.

ON

James .... to the head of department alone.

The gap can be filled with the words 'insisted on speaking', so you write:

Example:	**0**	INSISTED ON SPEAKING

Write **only** the missing words **IN CAPITAL LETTERS on the separate answer sheet**.

---

25 Ben married his fiancée without his parents' knowledge.

UNAWARE

Ben's .... his marriage to his fiancée.

26 The help-desk service is not, as many people believe, restricted to customers who buy products from the company directly.

COMMONLY

The help-desk service is not, ... , restricted to customers who buy products from the company directly.

27 Jane didn't feel like going to her sister's party.

MOOD

Jane wasn't .... to her sister's party.

28 My friends and I are looking for alternative accommodation because our apartment building is being pulled down.

ELSE

My friends and I are looking for .... live because our apartment building is being pulled down.

29 Peter's colleagues didn't realise how significant the research he was doing for his PhD was.

FAILED

Peter's colleagues .... of the research he was doing for his PhD.

30 'Did our sales figures get better last month, Martha?'

ANY

'Was .... our sales figures last month, Martha?'

Part 5

You are going to read an article in which a young journalist talks about using social media to find a job. For questions **31–36**, choose the answer (**A**, **B**, **C** or **D**) which you think fits best according to the text.

Mark your answers **on the separate answer sheet**.

Using Social Networking Sites to Find a Job

Having secured her own first job recently, Patty Meissner looks at young people's use of social networking when looking for work.

In many countries, a growing number of people in their twenties are turning to social media in the hope of finding work. Services like the social networking site Twitter and the professional networking site LinkedIn offer the chance for more direct contact with would-be employers than has previously been the case. But with greater access comes a greater chance to make mistakes.

Take the case of a young jobseeker in the US who contacted a senior marketing executive via LinkedIn. The marketing executive in question had an impressive list of influential people in her contact list; people whom the young jobseeker felt could help him land a job. The marketing executive, however, had other ideas. Indignant at the suggestion that she would willingly share a list of contacts painstakingly built up over many years with a complete stranger who'd done nothing to deserve such an opportunity, she not only rejected his contact request, but sent a vicious and heavily sarcastic rejection note that has since gone viral. Those who saw the note online were appalled, and the sender probably now regrets the tone of her note, if not the message it conveyed. But if the incident makes young people think more carefully about how they use social media in a professional capacity, she may have actually ended up doing them a favour. She has drawn attention to an unfortunate truth. Social media is a potentially dangerous tool for job hunters who don't know how to use it. And a worrying number are getting it wrong.

There's a horrible irony here, because in many countries social networking sites like Facebook and Twitter have been the bread and butter of twenty-somethings' social lives for years. When my generation were teenagers, social media was our escape from the prying eyes of parents and teachers. It was a cyber extension of the playground pecking order – a place to impress, to embellish and experiment. It was a world based largely on fantasy. You could find yourself in a three-hour conversation with someone online and then completely ignore them at school. With careful picture/song selection for your Facebook page, you could become a completely different and much more intriguing person overnight. And if you couldn't be bothered with conversation, 'poking' people on Facebook was a legitimate alternative.

However, when it comes to using social media for professional networking, our very knowledge and experience of sites like Facebook may actually be a hindrance. Using social media in a professional capacity is a completely different ball game, but for some twenty-somethings, the division is not clear cut. We first earned our online presence by being bold and over-confident, which could explain why some of us still come across like this. Just because a lot of people 'liked' your posts on Facebook, it doesn't mean you'll be able to use LinkedIn to show potential employers that you're someone worth employing. We need to realise that what we learned about social networking as teenagers no longer applies, and we must live up to employers' standards if we want to get on in the world of work.

One of the most common complaints from employers regarding young jobseekers on professional networking sites is that they're over-familiar in their form of address, and appear arrogant. This serves to perpetuate older generations' perceptions of us as an 'entitled generation'. In fact, we're very far from this; in many countries we're increasingly desperate about finding employment, which is why many of us are turning to social media in the first place. This impression of arrogance hurts the employment prospects of young people who – despite their communication errors – actually possess the skills and drive to become a valuable part of the workforce.

So what's the right way to contact someone on a professional networking site? Firstly, explain clearly who you are, and let the person you're writing to know what's in it for them – maybe you could offer to do a piece of research for them, or assist in some other way. This approach gives you a much better chance of getting a useful reply. Refrain from sending impersonal, blanket emails, and keep the tone humble if you want to avoid leaving a sour taste in the recipient's mouth. Remember – social media can be a great way to make useful contacts, but it needs careful handling if you don't want the door slammed in your face.

31 How did the senior marketing executive feel about the jobseeker who contacted her?

    A annoyed by the timing of his message
    B regretful that she had to reject his request
    C furious at his assumption of her cooperation
    D surprised that he offered her nothing in return

32 What does the writer say about the senior marketing executive?

    A Her note was an attempt to gain publicity.
    B Her attitude is not unusual on social networking sites.
    C She has unintentionally helped those looking for work.
    D Someone of her experience should treat jobseekers better.

33 What point does the writer make about social networking sites as used by her own generation?

    A They gave teenagers the impression that real conversation wasn't necessary.
    B Teenagers used them to avoid having to engage with people they didn't like.
    C They gave teenagers the chance to escape from their boring lives.
    D The personalities and relationships teenagers had on them didn't reflect reality.

34 As regards professional networking, the writer believes that many people of her generation

    A have exaggerated opinions of their own employability.
    B over-estimate the use of social media in the world of work.
    C fail to distinguish between social networking for pleasure and for work.
    D are unaware of the opportunities that professional networking sites can offer them.

35 In the fifth paragraph, the writer says that young jobseekers feel

    A certain that they are entitled to good jobs.
    B concerned that they may not be offered work.
    C certain that they have the ability to be useful as employees.
    D concerned that they are giving the wrong impression to employers.

36 What does the writer advise jobseekers to do?

    A tell prospective employers what they may gain in return
    B research the recipient carefully before they make contact
    C give careful consideration to the type of work they are seeking
    D approach only people they have a real chance of hearing back from

Part 6

You are going to read four extracts from articles in which experts give their views on climate change. For questions **37–40**, choose from the experts **A–D**. The experts may be chosen more than once.

Mark your answers **on the separate answer sheet**.

Can We Reduce Climate Change?

*Four experts give their views on whether it is possible
to mitigate the effects of global climate change.*

A The extreme weather conditions experienced in recent years are a clear indication that global warming is underway, and that future climate patterns will certainly follow the trajectory predicted unless measures are taken to lessen the impact of fossil fuel use. And yet the scenario is not as hopeless as many fear. Figures show that nations which are undergoing rapid economic growth are indeed causing a sizeable upsurge in global greenhouse gas (GHG) emissions at the present time. However, the GHG per person of these regions is currently still far below that of much of the world, and with their adoption of increasingly efficient technologies, it is unlikely that their GHG per person will ever equal that of Europe or North America. Indeed, my view is that the growing pace of scientific advancement will eventually find the means to mitigate and even reverse the consequences of climate change.

B There is no doubt that increasing industrialisation has had a measurable impact on GHG emissions, with consequences for climate and the environment. As for the future, however, even the most expert calculations are no more than speculation. What is more, even if the situation were to reach the catastrophic proportions that some foresee, this will not herald the end of life on earth as we know it. There have been many great climatic variations throughout history, and life forms have always adapted and survived. I see no reason why this period of change should be any different. And in the shorter term, it seems likely that GHG emissions will soon stabilise. The technologies to harness wind, wave and solar power have been in place for many years now, and as oil and gas become ever scarcer, markets will inevitably switch to more efficient and renewable resources.

C Despite recommendations from the Intergovernmental Panel on Climate Change, only a handful of countries have achieved any reduction in GHG emissions in recent years, while many developing countries have massively increased their fossil fuel use and hence their GHG emissions. It also seems probable that these levels will go on rising for decades, eclipsing any potential reductions elsewhere in the world. And while some sceptics question the accuracy of climate change forecasting, one cannot ignore the fact that most models produce strikingly similar results. This, to my mind, is evidence enough that something should be done. The potential consequences of failing to heed the warning signs is another question entirely. Even if it is too late to reverse the effects of global warming, I believe that the natural environment, and all its complex relationships, may eventually modify to cope with the changes. The earth is more resilient than we think.

D One only has to look at the world's GHG levels to realise that climate change is a real and urgent issue. Forecasts made in previous decades – anticipating hurricanes, floods and record temperatures – have proved correct, indicating that models of future trends are also likely to be accurate. Countries becoming newly industrialised are producing GHG emissions to such an extent as to erode all other countries' efforts to stabilise the world's temperature. This situation is likely to continue for some years yet. Thus, from melting polar caps to devastated rainforests and rising sea levels, our environment and the ecosystems they support are in grave danger. The key to averting potential catastrophe, I feel, lies in human ingenuity. For example, more efficient coal power stations already generate a third less emissions than conventional ones. Man has engineered this situation, and has the capacity – and incentive – to devise inventions to confront it.

Which expert

expresses a different opinion from C about the extent to which fossil fuels will continue to be used?

37	

has a different view from D on the contribution of developing countries to climate change?

38	

holds a different view from all the other experts on the reliability of climate change predictions?

39	

has the same view as B about whether ecosystems will adjust to the consequences of climate change?

40	

Part 7

You are going to read a magazine article about rock climbing. Six paragraphs have been removed from the article. Choose from the paragraphs **A–G** the one which fits each gap (**41–46**). There is one extra paragraph which you do not need to use.

Mark your answers **on the separate answer sheet**.

Impossible Rock

On the northern coast of Oman, climbers test themselves against knife-edge cliffs

We're standing on a pebble beach in northern Oman with a group of local men who are fishing. Behind us rises a sheer 1,000-metre cliff that shimmers under a blistering midday sun. 'Do you mind if I look around?' Alex asks. 'You can do as you please,' says the elder. As Alex wanders off, we explain to the Althouri fishermen that we're professional rock climbers on an exploratory visit.

41

There are six of us in our team, including Alex, one of the best young climbers in the world. Suddenly one of the men stops in his tracks, points up at the towering cliff, and starts shouting. A thousand feet above us Alex is climbing, antlike, up the rock wall. The Althouris are beside themselves with a mix of excitement and incredulity.

42

In 28 years of climbing I've never seen rock formations as magical. In places the land rises straight from the ocean in knife-edged fins. Proximity to the sea makes these cliffs perfect for deepwater soloing, a specialized type of climbing in which you push up as far a wall as you can, then simply tumble into the water. It sounds harmless enough, but an out-of-control fall can result in serious injury or even death.

43

Wasting no time, Alex laces up his climbing shoes, dives from the boat, and swims to a cliff where the ocean has carved out a cavern with a five-metre overhang. Within minutes he has reached the cavern's ceiling, where he finds a series of tiny hand holds along a protruding rib of dark grey limestone. It's exactly the kind of challenge he has been looking for, with every move more difficult than the one before.

44

'Come on!' I scream, urging him to finish his new route. Alex lunges over the lip, but his legs swing out, and he peels off the rock and leaps into the water. That night we anchor in the bay at the base of a 150-metre Gothic tower we dub the 'sandcastle'. Before joining Alex for the climb the next morning, I suggest we take along safety gear. The young climber scoffs, saying that it's nothing more than a hike. I think of myself as a young 44-year-old, but trying to keep up with him makes me realise how old I'm getting.

45

And now I'm slightly annoyed again about his disregard for whether I'm comfortable. The rock here is badly shattered, what climbers call choss. Clinging to the dead-vertical wall, I test the integrity of each hold by banging it with the heel of my hand. Sometimes the rock sounds hollow or even moves. Staring down between my legs, I see the boat bobbing in the bay far beneath us. By the time I plop down on the ledge beside him, my nerves are frazzled.

46

As I turn to my youthful partner for his thoughts, I see he's already packed up. For him the moment of wonder has passed. 'Let's go,' Alex says impatiently. 'If we hurry, we can get in another climb before dark.'

A From there we sail toward the 'Lion's Mouth,' a narrow strait named for the fang-like red and orange limestone pillars that jut from an overhang at its entrance. Alex spends the day working on a 60-metre route up one of the pillars.

B 'What are they saying?' I ask our translator. 'It's hard to explain,' he replies. 'But essentially, they think Alex is a witch.' I can understand why. Even for me, Alex's skills are hard to grasp. But so is this landscape.

C The claw-like fingers of the Musandam Peninsula below glow orange with the setting sun. Looking down at the tortuous shoreline, which fans out in every direction, we're gazing at a lifetime's worth of climbing.

D One of the other places we thought would be perfect for visiting by boat is As Salamah, an island in the Strait of Hormuz. We arrive in early afternoon and discover a giant rock rising from the sea. Since there is nowhere to anchor, we drop the sails and use the engines to park the boat just offshore.

E I'd already had a similar moment of awareness earlier in the trip when Alex had scampered up a 500-metre wall with our rope in his pack. 'Hold on a second!' I'd yelled. What if the rest of us needed it? 'Don't worry,' he'd replied. 'I'll stop when I think we need to start using the ropes.'

F The men puff on the pipes and nod. The mountainous peninsula on which they live is an intricate maze of bays and fjords. Few climbers have ever touched its sheer limestone cliffs. We had learned of the area's potential from some British climbers who visited ten years ago.

G Some defy belief. Hanging upside down, holding on to bumps in the rock no bigger than matchboxes, Alex hooks the heels of his sticky-soled shoes over a small protrusion. Defying gravity, he lets go with one hand and snatches for the next hold. Then the rock becomes too slick for a heel hook so he dangles his legs and swings like a chimpanzee from one tiny ledge to the next.

Part 8

You are going to read an article about risk taking. For questions **47–56**, choose from the sections **(A–D)**. The sections may be chosen more than once.

Mark your answers **on the separate answer sheet**.

Which section includes

the use of car imagery to help explain neural activity?	47
mention of one person's interest in the history of risk taking?	48
details of the process used to investigate the brain's mechanics?	49
a chemical-based explanation as to why people have such varied attitudes towards risk taking?	50
a well-known theory that explains why people take risks during everyday activities?	51
specific examples of what a person could lose if risk taking goes wrong?	52
mention of a common confusion about the chemical causes of risky behaviour?	53
a judgement of another person's stated belief about risk taking?	54
a reference to the fact that some people become addicted to the chemical reaction experienced in risk taking?	55
a description of a biological process initiated by fear in humans?	56

The Mystery of Risk

Jodie O'Rourke reviews current thinking about what lies behind risk taking

A Exploration of all sorts is rooted in the notion of taking risks. Risk underlies any journey into the unknown, whether it is a ship captain's voyage into uncharted seas, a scientist's research on dangerous diseases, or an entrepreneur's investment in a new venture. Some of the motivations for taking risks are obvious – financial reward, fame, political gain, saving lives. But as the danger increases, the number of people willing to go forward shrinks, until the only ones who remain are the extreme risk takers. This is the mystery of risk: what makes some humans willing to jeopardize their reputation, fortune, and life and to continue to do so, even in the face of dire consequences? Scientists have now begun to open up the neurological black box containing the mechanisms for risk taking and tease out the biological factors that may prompt someone to become an explorer. Their research has centred on neurotransmitters, the chemicals that control communication in the brain.

B One neurotransmitter that is crucial to the risk taking equation is dopamine, which helps control motor skills but also helps drive us to seek out and learn new things as well as process emotions such as anxiety and fear. Robust dopamine production holds one of the keys to understanding risk taking, says Larry Zweifel, a neurobiologist at the University of Washington. 'When you're talking about someone who takes risks to accomplish something, that's driven by motivation, and motivation is driven by the dopamine system. This is what compels humans to move forward.' Dopamine helps elicit a sense of satisfaction when we accomplish tasks: the riskier the task, the larger the hit of dopamine. Part of the reason we don't all climb mountains is that we don't all have the same amount of dopamine. Molecules on the surface of nerve cells called autoreceptors control how much dopamine we make and use, essentially controlling our appetite for risk.

C In a study conducted at Vanderbilt University, participants underwent scans allowing scientists to observe the autoreceptors in the part of the brain circuitry associated with reward, addiction, and movement. People who had fewer autoreceptors – that is, who had freer flowing dopamine – were more likely to engage in novelty-seeking behaviour, such as exploration. 'Think of dopamine like gasoline,' says neuropsychologist David Zald, the study's lead author. 'You combine that with a brain equipped with a lesser ability to put on the brakes than normal, and you get people who push limits.' This is where the discussion often mixes up risk takers with thrill seekers or adrenaline junkies. The hormone adrenaline is designed to help us escape from danger. It works like this: When the brain perceives a threat, it triggers the release of adrenaline into the bloodstream, which in turn stimulates the heart, lungs, muscles, and other parts of the body to help us flee or fight in a life-threatening situation. This release generates a feeling of exhilaration that continues after the threat has passed, as the adrenaline clears from the system. For some people, that adrenaline rush can become a reward the brain seeks. They are prompted to induce it by going to scary movies or engaging in extreme sports.

D Acclimating to risk is something we all do in our daily lives. A good example of this occurs when learning to drive a car. At first, a new driver may fear traveling on freeways, but over time that same driver with more experience will merge casually into speeding traffic with little consideration for the significant potential dangers. What is commonly referred to as the 'familiarity principle' can also be applied to help explain the lack of fear associated with high-risk situations. By practising an activity, humans can become used to the risk and manage the fear that arises in those situations. The notion that we are all descended from risk takers fascinates writer Paul Salopek. 'Early humans leaving the Great Rift Valley in Africa thousands of years ago were the first great explorers,' he reasons. 'At our innermost core we are all risk takers. And this shared willingness to explore our planet has bound our species from the very beginning.' It's a noble idea, albeit a dopamine-based one!

WRITING (1 hour 30 minutes)

Part 1

You **must** answer this question. Write your answer in **220–260** words in an appropriate style.

1   Your class has watched a television programme on the reasons why many young people choose to live in cities. You have made the notes below:

Factors which influence why many young people prefer to live in cities:
- work
- education
- culture

Some opinions expressed in the discussion:

"There are a greater range of jobs available in cities."

"Most universities are in big cities."

"There is so much happening in big cities."

Write an essay discussing **two** of the factors in your notes which influence why many young people choose to live in cities. You should **identify which factor you think is more significant, providing reasons** to support your opinion.

You may, if you wish, make use of the opinions expressed in the discussion, but you should use your own words as far as possible.

Part 2

Write an answer to **one** of the questions **2–4** in this part. Write your answer in **220–260** words in an appropriate style.

2   You work for an international company. The manager of your department would like to improve the ways in which the department trains new staff. Write a report for your manager in which you comment on the strengths and weaknesses of the current training programme and suggest how it could be improved.

Write your **report**.

3   An electronics magazine has asked for reviews of apps that readers have used. Write a review for the magazine in which you briefly describe the functions of an app you use, commenting on its strengths and weaknesses.

Write your **review**.

4   You are the student representative of your international college in London. You would like to invite a group of students from your country to visit the college, and decide to write a proposal to the college principal. In your proposal you should suggest how long the students' visit should last and briefly describe what activities should be included. You should also explain the potential benefits of the visit to the college and its students.

Write your **proposal**.

LISTENING (approximately 40 minutes)

Part 1

You will hear three different extracts.

For questions **1–6**, choose the answer (**A**, **B** or **C**) which fits best according to what you hear. There are two questions for each extract.

Extract One

You hear a trainee teacher called Susanna talking to her tutor.

1 What point does the tutor make about a teacher's attitude?

    A A good teacher can put any subject across effectively.

    B Students will pick up on a teacher's commitment.

    C There's little point in a teacher trying to fake passion for a subject.

2 What is Susanna doing?

    A complaining about her students' lack of enthusiasm

    B proposing ways of making her subject more appealing

    C asking for ideas about exercises her students could do

Extract Two

You hear a student called Sam telling his friend Ella about a concert he's been to.

3 Sam is trying to

    A suggest how the visual impact could have been improved.

    B challenge Ella's preconceptions about the music.

    C persuade Ella to go to a similar one in the future.

4 In Sam's opinion, what makes the performer stand out?

    A the influence her academic background has on her music

    B the instinctive way she responds to her audience

    C the high level of stage presence she displays

Extract Three

You hear a woman telling her friend about new policies adopted by her company.

5   Staff have been planting trees in order to

    A promote a desirable image.

    B encourage a spirit of mutual co-operation.

    C compensate for environmental damage.

6   The company was surprised that its remote working initiative resulted in

    A more appreciative customers.

    B a better standard of new recruits.

    C a more motivated workforce.

Part 2

You will hear a scientist called Jim Weller giving a talk about some robots he has created and how they function like insects called termites. For questions **7–14**, complete the sentences with a word or short phrase.

Robots Like Termites

Jim says termites differ from bees in that a **(7)** ....

is not responsible for organising their building work.

Jim uses the word **(8)** .... to refer to the group of robots

he's created to function as independent units.

Jim observed termites depositing partially consumed **(0)** ....

in shared habitats, which activated a response from other termites.

Jim states that the robots receive **(10)** .... to help them correct any

errors they make.

Jim got a single robot to finish the construction of a **(11)** .... when publicly

demonstrating how simple structure building is performed.

Jim predicts that his robots will soon be able to move **(12)** .... into

position to help people cope with the threat of floods.

Jim compares both termites and his robots to brain cells, in that they all create a

superior form of **(13)** ....

A group of Turkish researchers has observed Jim's work in the hope of coming up with a

(14) .... they can learn from.

Part 3

You will hear an interview in which a historian called Mark Connor and a writer called Judith Monroe are talking about the history of the underground railway in London. For questions **15–20**, choose the answer (**A, B, C** or **D**) which fits best according to what you hear.

15   Mark says that the problems which led to the creation of the railway
  A   resulted from poor urban planning.
  B   were similar to those we have today.
  C   typified the thinking of their age.
  D   only had one possible solution.

16   Judith believes that the engineering methods used to make the first tunnel
  A   worked surprisingly quickly.
  B   were too basic to be efficient.
  C   caused a minimum amount of disruption.
  D   resulted in the loss of too many homes.

17   How does Mark feel about the public reaction when the first underground line opened?
  A   disappointed by their reluctance to go underground
  B   struck by their willingness to tolerate lengthy journeys
  C   amused by their unfounded fears
  D   impressed by their general enthusiasm

18   Judith and Mark both say that, during the early years of its construction, the railway
  A   created many jobs for people.
  B   had a big influence on urban development.
  C   inspired imitators all over the world.
  D   made national heroes of its developers.

19   Judith compares certain underground stations to a classic film in that
  A   they are designed in the style of a particular era.
  B   they give a feeling of being in a cinema.
  C   they are a product of the same creative vision.
  D   they give a similar sense of size and excitement.

20   What does Mark think about the railway map?
  A   It has come to represent the city.
  B   It can confuse people unfamiliar with its format.
  C   It encourages people to use the underground.
  D   It is well designed for something so inexpensive.

Part 4

You will hear five short extracts in which people are talking about visits they have made to museums.

TASK ONE

For questions **21–25**, choose from the list (**A–H**) each speaker's reason for visiting the museum.

TASK TWO

For questions **26–30**, choose from the list (**A–H**) what impressed each speaker most about the museum.

While you listen, you must complete both tasks.

A to record certain images	A the helpfulness of the staff
B to view a particular exhibit	B the relevance to local life
C to listen to a lecture	C the effective audio-guide
D to follow up on a recommendation	D the international appeal
E to check some data	E the diversity of the items on show
F to do some research	F the comprehensive information supplied
G to see recent renovations	G the opportunities for interaction
H to seek expert opinion	H the authentic reconstructions

Speaker 1	**21**		Speaker 1	**26**
Speaker 2	**22**		Speaker 2	**27**
Speaker 3	**23**		Speaker 3	**28**
Speaker 4	**24**		Speaker 4	**29**
Speaker 5	**25**		Speaker 5	**30**

SPEAKING (15 minutes)

There are two examiners. One (the interlocutor) conducts the test, providing you with the necessary materials and explaining what you have to do. The other examiner (the assessor) is introduced to you, but then takes no further part in the interaction.

Part 1 (2 minutes)

The interlocutor first asks you and your partner for some information about yourselves, then widens the scope of the questions by asking about e.g. your leisure activities, studies, travel and daily life. You are expected to respond to the interlocutor's questions and listen to what your partner has to say.

Part 2 (a one-minute 'long turn' for each candidate, plus a 30-second response from the second candidate)

You are each given the opportunity to talk for about a minute, and to comment briefly after your partner has spoken.

The interlocutor gives you a set of three pictures and asks you to talk about two of them for about one minute. It is important to listen carefully to the interlocutor's instructions. The interlocutor then asks your partner a question about your pictures and your partner responds briefly.

You are then given another set of pictures to look at. Your partner talks about these pictures for about one minute. This time the interlocutor asks you a question about your partner's pictures and you respond briefly.

Part 3 (4 minutes)

In this part of the test, you and your partner are asked to talk together. The interlocutor places a question and some text prompts on the table between you. This stimulus provides the basis for a discussion, after which you will need to make a decision on the topic in question. The interlocutor explains what you have to do.

Part 4 (5 minutes)

The interlocutor asks some further questions, which leads to a more general discussion of the topic you have discussed in Part 3. You may comment on your partner's answers if you wish.

Test 6

READING AND USE OF ENGLISH (1 hour 30 minutes)

Part 1

For questions **1–8**, read the text below and decide which answer (**A, B, C** or **D**) best fits each gap. There is an example at the beginning (**0**).
Mark your answers **on the separate answer sheet**.

Example:

0 A typical   **B** usual   **C** classic   **D** standard

0	A ▬	B ▭	C ▭	D ▭

Solar Power for Indian Villages

Gulab Devi looks like a **(0)** .... rural woman from Rajasthan in north-west India. She can neither read nor write, but is **(1)** .... a successful pioneer in the Barefoot Solar Engineering Project, a scheme **(2)** .... to bring solar power to hundreds of villages across India. The availability of solar power **(3)** .... women from the arduous task of searching for wood for fuel and also reduces their **(4)** .... to unhealthy wood smoke.

Gulab is her family's sole breadwinner. Her job as a solar engineer **(5)** .... making electronic circuits and chargers for solar lighting panels, and she and her family are able to live comfortably on her salary.

Most of the engineers in the scheme are women, and are trained at the Barefoot College **(6)** .... by social worker Bunker Roy. His **(7)** .... is to address problems by building on skills that people already have, and then place the solutions to their problems in their own hands. Early **(8)** .... are that the project is having a powerful impact on the lives of women like Gulab.

1 **A** furthermore   **B** besides   **C** nevertheless   **D** alternatively

2 **A** decided   **B** inspired   **C** proposed   **D** designed

3 **A** eases   **B** frees   **C** lightens   **D** lifts

4 **A** appearance   **B** liability   **C** exposure   **D** situation

5 **A** demands   **B** implies   **C** concerns   **D** involves

6 **A** set down   **B** set in   **C** set up   **D** set aside

7 **A** pursuit   **B** aim   **C** determination   **D** tendency

8 **A** signals   **B** hints   **C** suggestions   **D** indications

Part 2

For questions **9–16**, read the text below and think of the word which best fits each gap. Use only **one** word in each gap. There is an example at the beginning (**0**).

Write your answers **IN CAPITAL LETTERS on the separate answer sheet**.

Example: | **0** | H | A | V | I | N | G | | | | | | | | | | | | |

Are You Happy Where You Work?

Finding a job you love is the first step to being happy at work, but **(0)** …….. the right workplace environment is equally important. Creativity, hard work and bright ideas come **(9)** …….. positive, happy working environments in **(10)** …….. people are allowed the freedom to think, develop and express themselves. It's important for everyone to have **(11)** …….. own clearly-defined work space, even if the workplace adopts an 'open plan' style, as so many offices now **(12)** …….. . Relaxation areas where people meet to chat and discuss ideas during office hours are regarded **(13)** …….. particularly beneficial.

Adding plants to the working environment can also **(14)** …….. offices to life, since they increase oxygen levels, purify the air and can create a calming and more productive environment. Finally, the lighting **(15)** …….. be right, because it can have a huge effect on people's moods. If offices are too harshly lit, **(16)** …….. can result in anger and headaches and lead to a lack of concentration.

Part 3

For questions **17–24**, read the text below. Use the word given in capitals at the end of some of the lines to form a word that fits in the gap **in the same line**. There is an example at the beginning (**0**).

Write your answers **IN CAPITAL LETTERS on the separate answer sheet**.

Example:

| 0 | A | B | I | L | I | T | Y | | | | | | | | | | | |

Camels in the Arctic?

Camels are well known for their **(0)** .... to survive the heat of the	**ABLE**
desert; however, scientists have unearthed the fossilised remains	
of a giant camel that **(17)** .... the forests of the High Arctic	**HABIT**
more than three million years ago. The ancient beast was almost	
three metres in **(18)** .... , about a third bigger than its modern	**HIGH**
(19) .... , the Arabian camel. Remains of the animal were found	**DESCEND**
on Ellesmere Island, the most northerly and **(20)** .... island of the	**MOUNTAIN**
Canadian Arctic archipelago.	
(21) .... from previous expeditions have shown that the camel's	**FIND**
ancestors **(22)** .... in North America 45 million years ago, but this is	**ORIGIN**
the first evidence of camels so far north. According to Mike Buckley,	
a researcher who studied the latest remains, this ancestor of modern	
camels may already have developed some of the **(23)** .... that	**ADAPT**
helped it survive in harsh climates – the hump for fat **(24)** .... for	**STORE**
instance, the large flat feet ideal for either snow or sand, and the big	
eyes that perhaps helped when long, dark winters made visibility poor.	

Part 4

For questions **25–30**, complete the second sentence so that it has a similar meaning to the first sentence, using the word given. **Do not change the word given.** You must use between **three** and **six** words, including the word given. Here is an example (**0**).

Example:

0 James would only speak to the head of department alone.

ON

James .... to the head of department alone.

The gap can be filled with the words 'insisted on speaking', so you write:

Example: | **0** | | INSISTED ON SPEAKING |

Write **only** the missing words **IN CAPITAL LETTERS on the separate answer sheet**.

---

25 Your books will be despatched on receipt of your order provided they are in stock.

SOON

We will despatch your books .... the order provided they are in stock.

26 Because the gym increased its fees last month, I am no longer a member.

UP

If the gym .... its fees last month, I would still be a member.

27 The driver said that we were delayed because an earlier train had broken down.

CAUSED

According to the driver, our .... breakdown of an earlier train.

28 It was Sarah's ideas that enabled us to put on a successful fashion show.

FOR

If ………………………………... ideas, we wouldn't have been able to put on a successful fashion show.

29 Leo was the only person in the street who didn't come to my farewell party.

EXCEPTION

Everyone in the street ……………………………... to my farewell party.

30 The concert should have started about three hours ago.

DUE

The concert ……………………………... about three hours ago.

Part 5

You are going to read an article about the future of newspapers. For questions **31–36**, choose the answer (**A**, **B**, **C** or **D**) which you think fits best according to the text.
Mark your answers **on the separate answer sheet**.

The Future of Newspapers

Anybody who says they can reliably forecast the future of newspapers is either a liar or a fool. Look at the raw figures, and newspapers seem doomed. Since 2000, the circulation of most UK national dailies has fallen by between a third and a half. The authoritative Pew Research Centre in the USA reports that newspapers are now the main source of news for only 26 percent of US citizens as against 45 percent in 2001. There is no shortage of prophets who confidently predict that the last printed newspaper will be safely buried within 15 years at most.

Yet one of the few reliable facts of history is that old media have a habit of surviving. An over-exuberant New York journalist announced in 1835 that books and theatre 'have had their day' and the daily newspaper would become 'the greatest organ of social life'. Theatre duly withstood not only the newspaper, but also cinema
line 10 and then television. Radio has flourished in the TV age; cinema, in turn, has held its own against videos and DVDs. Even vinyl records have made a comeback, with online sales up 745 percent since 2008.

Newspapers themselves were once new media, although it took several centuries before they became the dominant medium for news. This was not solely because producing up-to-date news for a large readership over a wide area became practicable and economic only in the mid-19th century, with the steam press, the railway and the telegraph. Equally important was the emergence of the idea that everything around us is in constant movement and we need to be updated on its condition at regular intervals – a concept quite alien in medieval times and probably also to most people in the early modern era. Now, we expect change. To our medieval ancestors, however, the only realities were the passing of the seasons, punctuated by catastrophes such as famine, flood or disease that they had no reliable means of anticipating. Life, as the writer Alain de Botton puts it, was 'ineluctably cyclical' and 'the most important truths were recurring'.

Journalism as a full-time trade from which you could hope to make a living hardly existed before the 19th century. Even then, there was no obvious reason why most people needed news on a regular basis, whether daily or weekly. In some respects, regularity of newspaper publication and rigidity of format was, and remains, a burden. Online news readers can dip in and out according to how they perceive the urgency of events. Increasingly sophisticated search engines and algorithms allow us to personalise the news to our own priorities and interests. When important stories break, internet news providers can post minute-by-minute updates. Error, misconception and foolish speculation can be corrected or modified almost instantly. There are no space restrictions to prevent narrative or analysis, and documents or events cited in news stories can often be accessed in full. All this is a world away from the straitjacket of newspaper publication. Yet few if any providers seem alive to the new medium's capacity for spreading understanding and enlightenment.

Instead, the anxiety is always to be first with the news, to maximise reader comments, to create heat, sound and fury and thus add to the sense of confusion. In the medieval world, what news there was was usually exchanged amid the babble of the marketplace or the tavern, where truth competed with rumour, mishearing and misunderstanding. In some respects, it is to that world that we seem to be returning. Newspapers have never been very good – or not as good as they ought to be – at telling us how the world works. Perhaps they now face extinction. Or perhaps, as the internet merely adds to what de Botton describes as our sense that we live in 'an unimprovable and fundamentally chaotic universe', they will discover that they and they alone can guide us to wisdom and understanding.

31 In the first paragraph, the writer is presenting

    A his interpretation of a current trend.

    B evidence that supports a widespread view.

    C his prediction on the future of print journalism.

    D reasons for the decline in newspaper readership.

32 What point is the writer making in the second paragraph?

    A Existing media are not necessarily replaced by new ones.

    B The best media technologies tend to be the most long-lasting.

    C Public enthusiasm for new types of media is often unpredictable.

    D It is inevitable that most media technologies will have a limited life.

33 Which phrase in the second paragraph has the same meaning as 'held its own against' in line 10?

    A 'had their day'

    B 'withstood'

    C 'flourished'

    D 'made a comeback'

34 In the third paragraph, the writer stresses the significance of

    A a shift in people's attitudes towards the outside world.

    B certain key 19th-century advances in mechanisation.

    C the challenges of news distribution in the pre-industrial era.

    D the competition between newspapers and more established media.

35 What does the writer suggest is the main advantage of online news sites?

    A the flexibility of the medium

    B the accuracy of the reporting

    C the ease of access for their users

    D the breadth of their potential readership

36 What does the writer suggest about newspapers in the final paragraph?

    A They still have an important role to play.

    B They can no longer compete with the internet.

    C They will have to change to keep up with the digital age.

    D They will retain a level of popularity among certain types of readers.

Part 6

You are going to read extracts from four articles in which museum directors give their views on museums. For questions **37–40**, choose from the extracts **A–D**. The museum directors may be chosen more than once.

Mark your answers **on the separate answer sheet**.

Museums

A Statistics show that museums are going from strength to strength in terms of visitor numbers, which is an encouraging sign in our computer-obsessed society. Online access increasingly rules how we approach information today, and museums have to engage with this to stay relevant. That said, a picture on a screen cannot replace material engagement with an object. Unfortunately, many people still have rather outdated ideas of what museums are like, including believing that they are high-brow institutions aimed at some international elite, which is clearly no longer the case, particularly with the smaller ones. With effort, a museum can be the heart of a community, preserving the stories which are important to those who live nearby, and I know of many such museums all over the country which are thriving.

B It is interesting that people who do not think twice about visiting a museum when on holiday very rarely set foot in one the rest of the time, but this is nothing to do with a failure to accommodate a wide range of people – museums definitely do that nowadays. I think it is more that, when we are entrenched in our daily routine, museums are not high on our list of priorities. Breaking out of that routine gives you the opportunity to do different things, among them things like visiting museums. Part of the appeal of museums, of course, is the chance to view objects from around the world and get a taste of another culture. Although there are rigorous export controls stopping objects of national significance being sold abroad, thanks to the internet museums can co-operate to arrange reciprocal loans for special exhibitions.

C Museums are clearly keen to capitalise on the possibilities offered by the internet, and it is a valuable tool for extending access. Exhibitions can remain on view on our website indefinitely after a physical show has been dismantled, and people have the opportunity to examine fascinating artefacts and works of art from all corners of the globe in much greater detail than they can in the gallery. The only downside of the increasing expectation of online access that I can see, is that provincial museums lose out to the large nationals, as their more limited resources mean they cannot hope to compete. I am convinced that this is what is behind their falling visitor numbers. Having said that, on a national level, more people feel that museums are relevant to everyone, rather than just a select few, and this has clearly made a difference.

D I would love to think that people come through the door of institutions such as mine because they want to open their minds to new things, but, while that may be true of a few, I know that the majority are visitors to the city who are including one or two museums in their itinerary in order to add variety. Having said that, I really hope that they leave with a wish to come back, or to try other museums. I also think there is still a long way to go in terms of winning over visitors from less privileged backgrounds. In this age of fast-changing, user-friendly digital technology, many people feel intimidated by the rather dry, academic way in which many still display their exhibits. We are now working a great deal more with overseas museums, and, in addition to allowing us to constantly change the items we have on display, we have found that this encourages museums, and even governments, to engage in dialogue.

Which museum director

has a different opinion from C on the value of using digital media to present exhibits?	**37**
shares B's view on the further benefit of museums exhibiting objects from other countries?	**38**
has a different opinion from A about the success of local museums?	**39**
has a different opinion from the others about how well museums cater for all levels of society?	**40**

Part 7

You are going to read a magazine article about ways of reusing escaped heat. Six paragraphs have been removed from the article. Choose from the paragraphs **A–G** the one which fits each gap (**41–46**). There is one extra paragraph which you do not need to use.

Mark your answers **on the separate answer sheet.**

City of Heat

Escaped heat costs us money and affects our climate. Chelsea Wald reports on a grand plan to capture it and put it to good use.

Deep in the tunnels of London's underground railway, as in many around the world, it's so hot it can feel very uncomfortable. And yet in the basement of a building only a few metres away from the station a boiler is firing to heat water for someone's shower.

41

Recapturing it wouldn't just benefit our wallets. It would reverse some of the damaging effects on the climate. The good news is that several cities have found a way to hunt down their surplus heat in some unexpected places. These cities are building systems that deliver heat in much the same way that suppliers handle electricity and water. Could they point the way to the next energy revolution?

42

It was also estimated that given the right technologies, we could reclaim nearly half of that energy, although that's easier said than done. 'We often talk about the quantity of waste heat,' says David MacKay, chief scientific adviser to the UK Department of Energy and Climate Change, 'but not the quality.' Most of what we think of as 'waste heat' isn't actually all that hot; about sixty percent is below 230°C. While that may sound pretty hot, it is too cold to turn a turbine to generate electricity.

43

There, buildings tap into the system to warm their water supplies or air for central heating. Many countries are encouraging such cogeneration, as it is called. A US initiative, for example, might save the country $10 billion per year. And cogeneration allows power plants to bump up their efficiencies from thirty percent to almost ninety percent.

44

As it happens, there is an existing technology that can siphon energy from such temperatures, although applying it on a large scale to capture waste heat is as yet unachievable. Ground source heat pumps have been helping homeowners save on heating bills since the 1940s, when US inventor Robert Webber realised he could invert the refrigeration process to extract heat from the ground.

45

The mechanism for this is simple. A network of pipes makes a circuit between the inside of the dwelling and a coil buried underground. These pipes contain a mix of water and fluid refrigerant. As the fluid mixture travels through the pipes buried underground, it absorbs the heat from the 10°C soil.

46

This system is powerful enough to efficiently provide heat even in places as cold as Norway and Alaska. It is also cheap. Scientists around the world are now working on the idea that the way ahead is to develop city-wide grids using source-heat pumps to recycle waste on a grander scale, from sources such as subways and sewers.

A But that's not all it can do. Reverse the process and it can cool a home in summer. If the ground is cold enough, it simply absorbs the heat from inside the building instead of from the ground.

B It's an attractive proposition. A report in 2008 found that the energy lost as heat each year by US industry equalled the annual energy use of five million citizens. Power generation is a major culprit; the heat lost from that sector alone dwarfs the total energy use of Japan. The situation in other industrialised countries is similar.

C Yet even this is just a drop in the ocean compared with the heat lost from our homes, offices, road vehicles and trains. However, waste heat from these myriad sources is much harder to harness than the waste heat from single, concentrated sources like power plants. What's more, it's barely warm enough to merit its name. Reclaiming that would be an altogether more difficult proposition.

D A more successful way of using the heat is to move the heat directly to where it is needed. A number of power plants now do exactly that. They capture some or all of their waste heat and send it – as steam or hot water – through a network of pipes to nearby cities.

E The system takes advantage of the fact that in temperate regions – regardless of surface temperature – a few metres underground, the soil always remains lukewarm and stable. These pumps can tap into that consistent temperature to heat a house in the winter.

F While this is not what you might consider hot, it nonetheless causes the liquid to evaporate into a gas. When this gas circulates back into the building, it is fed through a compressor, which vastly intensifies the heat. That heat can then be used by a heat exchanger to warm up hot water or air ducts.

G Rather than stewing in that excess heat, what if we could make it work for us? Throughout our energy system – from electricity generation in power plants to powering a car – more than fifty percent of the energy we use leaks into the surroundings.

Part 8

You are going to read an article about the value of boredom. For questions **47–56**, choose from the sections (**A–D**). The sections may be chosen more than once.

Mark your answers **on the separate answer sheet**.

Which section

points out a drawback in failing to allow time for mundane reflection?	47
comments on a personal experience of using a particular psychological technique?	48
comments on the broad appeal that a particular notion might potentially have?	49
suggests that boredom **as a** way of dealing with a problem is not a new idea?	50
distinguishes between mere reflection and conscious avoidance of mental stimulation?	51
refers to the communication of an erroneous message?	52
refers to an activity indicative of modern life taking place in various locations?	53
outlines a positive consequence of distancing oneself from technology?	54
explains that a particular finding supported existing knowledge?	55
remarks on the significance of monotony in the development of the human species?	56

Time Out

It seems that embracing boredom and allowing ourselves to drift away could be good for us

A

Consider any public place where people used to enjoy a spot of silent contemplation – from train carriages and beauty spots to our local streets – and these days you'll see people plugged into their seductive electronic sources of constant stimulation. All this information overload seems like a terribly modern-day problem. But one unique thinker actually stumbled on a neat solution several decades ago: radical boredom. In 1942, a German writer called Siegfried Karcauer wrote despairingly of the massive over-stimulation of the modern city where people listening to the radio were in a state of 'permanent receptivity, constantly pregnant with London, the Eiffel Tower, Berlin.' His answer was to suggest a period of total withdrawal from stimulation – to cut ourselves off and experience 'extraordinary, radical boredom'. On a sunny afternoon when everyone is outside, one would do best to hang about the train station,' he wrote. 'Or better yet, stay at home, draw the curtains and surrender oneself to one's boredom on the sofa.'

B

Karcauer believed that actively pursuing boredom in this way was a valuable means of unlocking playful wild ideas far away from plain reality and, better still, achieve 'a kind of bliss that is almost unearthly'. It's a beautiful theory and one that would definitely hold an allure for many people. Plus modern research suggests that it might actually have a sound psychological basis. To test the potential positives of boredom, psychologist Dr Sandi Mann asked a group of 40 people to complete a task designed to showcase their creativity. But before they got started on it, a subgroup was asked to perform a suitably dull task – copying numbers from the telephone directory for 15 minutes. The data pointed to the group that had previously endured boredom displaying more creative flair during the task than the control group. According to psychologists this is normal, because when people become bored and start to daydream, their minds come up with different processes and they work out more creative solutions to problems.

C

This would suggest perhaps, that by over-stimulating our minds, we're not just making ourselves more stressed, we're also missing out on a chance to unhook our thoughts from the daily grind and think more creatively. Having said that, psychologists also point out that despite its bad reputation, boredom has a definite evolutionary purpose. Mann says 'Without it, we'd be like toddlers in a perpetual state of amazement. Just imagine it: "Wow – look at that fantastic cereal at the bottom of my bowl!" It may be very stimulating, but we'd never get anything done.' That puts me in mind of adults who are addicted to social media and smart phones – attention-seeking, scurrying around the internet screaming 'Look at this! Look at them! Look at me!' while the real world beyond the electronic devices continues on untroubled and unexamined. Meanwhile, as Mann points out, we're incorrectly teaching our actual toddlers that boredom and lack of stimulation is something to be feared rather than embraced.

D

So how do you learn to tactically embrace periods of radical boredom? The first step is realising that this is different from simply taking time to ponder what you've done since getting up that morning. 'Using boredom positively is about creating new opportunities when your mind isn't occupied and you can't focus on anything else,' says Mann. This could be as simple as staring out the window or watching the rain come down. Or heading off for a solitary walk with no fixed destination in mind, or your smart phone in your pocket. Anything that gives your mind the rare chance to drift off its moorings. 'I can really recommend it,' says Mann. 'It's a great experience – like taking a holiday from your brain.' I'm definitely sold. I'm trying to keep my phone turned off during the weekends and allow myself the odd, dreamy wallow on the sofa during the week, time permitting. And the best thing: it works. After taking a break and allowing my mind to roam, it returns refreshed and revitalized, with a fresh take on the challenges that I face during the day. When my daughter gets to an age when she's ready to whine 'I'm bored', I'll know exactly what to say!

WRITING (1 hour 30 minutes)

Part 1

You **must** answer this question. Write your answer in **220–260** words in an appropriate style.

---

1 Your class has had a discussion about the importance of stories for young children. You have made the notes below:

> **Ways in which stories for young children are important:**
> - entertainment
> - education
> - social values

> Some opinions expressed in the discussion:
>
> "Stories are fun."
>
> "Stories develop children's vocabulary."
>
> "Children find out the difference between right and wrong."

Write an essay for your tutor discussing **two** of the ways in which stories for young children are important from your notes. You should **explain which way you think is more important, providing reasons** for your opinion.

You may, if you wish, make use of the opinions expressed in the discussion, but you should use your own words as far as possible.

Part 2

Write an answer to **one** of the questions **2–4** in this part. Write your answer in **220–260** words in an appropriate style.

---

2   You have been studying at your international college for a year. The Principal of the college has asked you to write a report about the study resources offered to students, suggesting ways in which these resources could be improved for next year.

Write your **report**.

3   You have recently been on an activity holiday and decide to write a review of the holiday for a travel magazine. In your review, describe the particular activity holiday, and evaluate to what extent it met your expectations and whether you would encourage other people to try this kind of holiday.

Write your **review**.

4   The company you work for is considering the idea of a flexible working day, where staff are able to vary their starting and finishing time. The manager of your department has asked you to write a proposal explaining why introducing a flexible working day would benefit both the company and its employees. You should also suggest how a flexible working day could operate in your own department.

Write your **proposal**.

LISTENING (approximately 40 minutes)

Part 1

You will hear three different extracts.

For questions **1–6**, choose the answer (**A**, **B** or **C**) which fits best according to what you hear. There are two questions for each extract.

Extract One

You hear a sportsman and a businesswoman discussing the issue of being competitive.

1 How does the man feel about the book he's read on competitiveness?

    A surprised that it contradicts a well-established theory

    B confused by the wide range of evidence it quotes

    C unsure about certain aspects of its argument

2 The woman feels that in the business world, prioritising competitiveness leads to

    A a demotivating effect on the workforce.

    B a constant drive towards greater productivity.

    C an obsession with short-term goals.

Extract Two

You hear two friends discussing some research into the impact of colour on memory.

3 They both say that

    A restaurants use clever tactics to attract new customers.

    B the research methods used seem valid.

    C the same colours can affect people in different ways.

4 The woman feels that the teenager's findings

    A could prove significant in the long-term.

    B need the backing of the scientific establishment.

    C confirm initial evidence about the way memory is viewed.

Extract Three

You hear two people discussing a television programme about music and the effect it has on the brain.

5   How does the woman feel about the programme?

    A   surprised by its conclusion

    B   confused by the approach it took

    C   disappointed by the lack of explanation

6   What do they agree about music?

    A   It has unexpected benefits.

    B   Its effects on intelligence are obvious.

    C   It's important to study its psychological impact.

Part 2

You will hear a radio report by the journalist Susie Stubbs, who has been to the tropical island of Réunion to find out about the flavouring called vanilla. For questions **7–14**, complete the sentences with a word or short phrase.

Vanilla

Susie says that, despite its cost, vanilla is the world's most **(7)** .... spice.

The vanilla plant is originally from Mexico, where it depends on a local

(8) .... for its existence.

Susie says the term **(9)** .... is used to talk about vanilla plants on the island.

Recently the vanilla harvest has been affected by

(10) .... and this impacts on the price.

These days the vanilla plants are covered by **(11)** .... for protection.

Sometimes there are **(12)** .... in the vanilla seed pods to show which

farm they come from.

The vanilla pods are sun-dried and then

(13) .... briefly before being packed in boxes.

The boxes used to store the pods are wrapped in **(14)** .... to keep the heat in.

Part 3

You will hear a radio interview in which two young journalists – called Angus Brown and Yolanda Zouche – are talking about their work. For questions **15–20**, choose the answer (**A**, **B**, **C** or **D**) which fits best according to what you hear.

---

15   In Yolanda's opinion, what is the most challenging aspect of her job?
   A   finding suitable images to accompany articles
   B   trying to locate interviewees
   C   expressing herself coherently within a tight word limit
   D   working to demanding time constraints

16   What is it about their work that Angus and Yolanda both enjoy?
   A   the variety of the projects they get involved in
   B   the challenge of reporting news effectively
   C   the opportunity to meet interesting people
   D   the appeal of searching out information

17   In Angus's opinion, the advantage of online newspapers over print versions is that they
   A   are able to cover a greater range of topics.
   B   can keep up with events as they develop.
   C   allow interaction by readers.
   D   reach a far wider public.

18   What made getting a job in journalism so hard for Angus?
   A   the extent of competition for posts
   B   a low level of encouragement from others
   C   a lack of previous professional experience
   D   the difficulty of establishing useful contacts

19   Yolanda believes that the essential requirement for a journalist entering the profession is
   A   an ability to write persuasively.
   B   a clear and logical mind.
   C   a resourceful and confident character.
   D   a mastery of interviewing techniques.

20   Angus's recommendation for aspiring journalists is to
   A   cultivate an interest in a specific field.
   B   seize every opportunity to express themselves in writing.
   C   concentrate on developing a distinct style.
   D   become a keen observer of life around them.

Part 4

You will hear five short extracts in which people are talking about strategies they've adopted for handling work-related problems.

TASK ONE

For questions **21–25**, choose from the list (**A–H**) why each speaker decided to adopt their particular strategy.

TASK TWO

For questions **26–30**, choose from the list (**A–H**) how each speaker felt after implementing the strategy.

While you listen, you must complete both tasks.

A angry at the incompetence of colleagues	
B delighted by an unexpected benefit	Speaker 1 [26]
C upset by an unsympathetic response	Speaker 2 [27]
D amused by a coincidence	Speaker 3 [28]
E optimistic at the prospect of future success	Speaker 4 [29]
F disappointed because of a misunderstanding	Speaker 5 [30]
G puzzled by people's reactions	
H envious of the ability of others	

A to strengthen a relationship	
B to reassure an employer	Speaker 1 [21]
C to help deal with extensive responsibilities	Speaker 2 [22]
D to meet the demands of colleagues	Speaker 3 [23]
E to cope with unpredictability	Speaker 4 [24]
F to avoid unfair criticism	Speaker 5 [25]
G to fulfil public expectations	
H to get some personal space	

SPEAKING (15 minutes)

There are two examiners. One (the interlocutor) conducts the test, providing you with the necessary materials and explaining what you have to do. The other examiner (the assessor) is introduced to you, but then takes no further part in the interaction.

Part 1 (2 minutes)

The interlocutor first asks you and your partner for some information about yourselves, then widens the scope of the questions by asking about e.g. your leisure activities, studies, travel and daily life. You are expected to respond to the interlocutor's questions and listen to what your partner has to say.

Part 2 (a one-minute 'long turn' for each candidate, plus a 30-second response from the second candidate)

You are each given the opportunity to talk for about a minute, and to comment briefly after your partner has spoken.

The interlocutor gives you a set of three pictures and asks you to talk about two of them for about one minute. It is important to listen carefully to the interlocutor's instructions. The interlocutor then asks your partner a question about your pictures and your partner responds briefly.

You are then given another set of pictures to look at. Your partner talks about these pictures for about one minute. This time the interlocutor asks you a question about your partner's pictures and you respond briefly.

Part 3 (4 minutes)

In this part of the test, you and your partner are asked to talk together. The interlocutor places a question and some text prompts on the table between you. This stimulus provides the basis for a discussion, after which you will need to make a decision on the topic in question. The interlocutor explains what you have to do.

Part 4 (5 minutes)

The interlocutor asks some further questions, which leads to a more general discussion of the topic you have discussed in Part 3. You may comment on your partner's answers if you wish.

Test 7

READING AND USE OF ENGLISH (1 hour 30 minutes)

Part 1

For questions **1–8**, read the text below and decide which answer (**A, B, C** or **D**) best fits each gap.
There is an example at the beginning (**0**).
Mark your answers **on the separate answer sheet**.

Example:

0 A item **B** article **C** piece **D** unit

0	A	B	C	D
	▢	▢	▬	▢

Changing Typefaces

In what can only be described as an impressive **(0)** …….. of research, a schoolboy in the USA has calculated that the state and federal governments could save getting on for $400m a year by changing the typeface they use for printed documents.

Shocked by the number of printed handouts he was receiving from his teachers, the 14-year-old boy decided to investigate the cost. He established that ink **(1)** …….. up to 60% of the cost of a printed page and is, gram for gram, twice as expensive as some famous perfumes. He then started looking at the different typefaces and discovered that, by **(2)** …….. to one called Garamond with its thin, elegant strokes, his school district could reduce its ink **(3)** …….. by 24% annually. Working on that **(4)** …….. , the federal savings would be enormous.

(5) …….. , earlier studies of the **(6)** …….. of font choice have shown that it can affect more than just cost. The typeface that a document uses also **(7)** …….. how much of the information is **(8)** …….. and whether it is worth taking seriously.

1 **A** represents   **B** measures   **C** equals   **D** indicates

2 **A** varying   **B** modifying   **C** adapting   **D** switching

3 **A** application   **B** intake   **C** capacity   **D** consumption

4 **A** belief   **B** basis   **C** impression   **D** thought

5 **A** Fundamentally **B** Seemingly   **C** Interestingly **D** Unusually

6 **A** issue   **B** concern   **C** aspect   **D** discussion

7 **A** guides   **B** rules   **C** dominates   **D** influences

8 **A** preserved   **B** retained   **C** accumulated   **D** gathered

Part 2

For questions **9–16**, read the text below and think of the word which best fits each gap. Use only **one** word in each gap. There is an example at the beginning (**0**).

Write your answers **IN CAPITAL LETTERS on the separate answer sheet**.

Example:

0	U	N	D	E	R													

My First Paddle-Boarding Lesson

Here I am in a cold, windy city, **(0)** .... a very grey sky. I ask myself **(9)** .... I'm standing on an oversized surfboard in the middle of a river with nothing to help me **(10)** .... a paddle. I'm about to have my first lesson in paddle-boarding, which is a bit **(11)** .... canoeing but with only one paddle and, being upright, you can enjoy the views on offer. The teacher reassures me it's easy, which **(12)** .... nothing to reduce the pressure. I desperately try to keep **(13)** .... balance and concentrate on not falling in. I wonder if I've left it too late to back out and head for solid ground, but before I can change my mind I'm **(14)** .... the move, but not going where I want to. I hear my teacher shouting 'Paddle paddle'; I try but, **(15)** .... my best efforts, I don't make much progress. 'You need to paddle on both sides,' he says, 'because **(16)** .... you'll go around in circles. Copy me.' And finally I'm moving in the same direction as everyone else and it feels amazing.

Part 3

For questions **17–24**, read the text below. Use the word given in capitals at the end of some of the lines to form a word that fits in the gap **in the same line**. There is an example at the beginning **(0)**.

Write your answers **IN CAPITAL LETTERS on the separate answer sheet**.

Example: | 0 | D | E | A | L | I | N | G | S | | | | | | | | | |

The Joy of Mathematics

Are you good at maths? Many people would say 'no'. They have no

confidence in their **(0)** .... with numbers. Maths lessons at school   **DEAL**

are remembered as hours of **(17)** .... rather than enjoyment, and   **ENDURE**

this memory is **(18)** .... what colours their attitude to maths in   **DOUBT**

adulthood.

But in some ways, society is **(19)** .... of this attitude. We accept   **TOLERATE**

without question the need to be literate, so why isn't numeracy valued

in the same way? For those who loathe maths, there seem to be

(20) .... psychological barriers preventing them from appreciating   **MASS**

the **(21)** .... of maths to our everyday lives.   **USE**

But all is not lost. A professor of maths in the USA has set up a

blog that aims to make maths **(22)** .... to those who missed out   **ACCESS**

at school and to remove the many **(23)** .... that some people have   **ANXIOUS**

about the subject. He wants to share some of his enthusiasm for

maths, and by introducing people to the beauty of maths, **(24)** ....   **HOPE**

make it a more joyful experience.

Part 4

For questions **25–30**, complete the second sentence so that it has a similar meaning to the first sentence, using the word given. **Do not change the word given.** You must use between **three** and **six** words, including the word given. Here is an example (**0**).

Example:

0 James would only speak to the head of department alone.

ON

James .... to the head of department alone.

The gap can be filled with the words 'insisted on speaking', so you write:

Example:	**0**	INSISTED ON SPEAKING

Write **only** the missing words **IN CAPITAL LETTERS on the separate answer sheet**.

---

25 The biographer decided to leave out all the less interesting details of the footballer's childhood.

ANY

The biographer decided not .... the less interesting details of the footballer's childhood.

26 David apologised for being unable to come to the meeting next week.

COULD

David said he .... come to the meeting next week.

27 Since starting her new job, Charlotte has completely forgotten about the plans she used to have.

SIGHT

Since starting her new job, Charlotte has completely .... the plans she used to have.

28 I can never remember dates for anything, even though I really try.

MATTER

I can never remember dates for anything …………………………….…... try.

29 The impression his boss has of Jack is that he's an ambitious person.

ACROSS

Jack ……………………………….…... an ambitious person.

30 Casper didn't mention the fact that we had met before.

REFERENCE

Casper ……………………………….…... the fact that we had met before.

Part 5

You are going to read an internet article about a work policy of unlimited leave time. For questions **31–36**, choose the answer (**A**, **B**, **C** or **D**) which you think fits best according to the text. Mark your answers **on the separate answer sheet**.

Unlimited Time Off Work
Barnaby Spence considers a new idea from the world of big business

The founder of a multinational corporation recently announced that his company would no longer be keeping track of its employees' paid holiday time. The move was apparently inspired by an internet company which has instigated a similar policy. According to the founder of the multinational corporation, the idea came to him via a cheery email (reproduced in many newspapers) from his daughter. In it she sounds suspiciously like a copywriter from her father's media team. Setting aside the fact that the means by which the announcement was made seems like a hollow attempt at 'humanising' what may turn out to be a less than generous policy decision, let us ask: is the idea practical?

The internet company and the multinational corporation are fundamentally distinct – the former has 2,000 employees and provides a single service, while the latter has 50,000 employees with dozens of subsidiary companies providing services as diverse as financial services, transport, and healthcare. The approach of 'take as much time off as you want as long as you're sure it won't damage the business' seems better suited to a smaller company where employees have a better idea of each other's workloads and schedules, and so may be more comfortable in assessing whether their absence would harm the business – in any case a problematically abstract notion.

The founder of the multinational has stated that his employees may take as much leave as they want, as long as they 'feel a hundred percent comfortable that they and their team are up to date on every project and that their absence will not in any way damage the business – or, for that matter, their careers.' Is it possible to be that sure? No matter how many loose ends you manage to tie up in advance of a holiday, there is always a mountain of work to come back to. That is simply the nature of leave; you put your work on hold, but its accumulation is inevitable and beyond your control. Someone who follows these guidelines would likely not go at all, or, at the very least, would feel overly guilty about going. Increased levels of guilt lead to stress and this, together with workers not taking sufficient leave, would lead to a decrease in productivity in the long run.

The situation could be compounded by pressure from colleagues and office gossip concerning who was off when, and for how long. Such pressure already affects decisions such as when to start and end the working day. Particularly in the corporate sector, there is a culture of working late, and it is easy to see how this could translate into a 'no holiday' culture in a company with unlimited leave, where workers compete for promotion. Similarly, if the feelings of safety and entitlement that statutory leave provides are removed, people may feel unable to take the leave they require for fear of appearing lazy. Essentially, they would no longer have their legal entitlement to fall back on. Perhaps then, the policy would result in a sort of paralysis, where workers did not feel able to take their entitled leave, or, they might continue to use their statutory rights as a guideline, leaving the policy obsolete.

Modern technology, which allows us to receive work messages whenever and wherever we are, has blurred the distinction between work and leisure time. The internet company apparently began their unlimited leave policy when their employees asked how this new way of working could be reconciled with the company's old-fashioned time-off policy. That is to say, if their employer was no longer able to accurately track employees' total time on the job, why should it apply a different and outmoded standard to their time away from it? However, a potentially problematic corollary of having no set working hours is that all hours are feasibly working hours. Employees can never be sure whether or not their working hours are being monitored by their employer, causing them to internalise this scrutiny and become self-disciplining, with possibly destructive effects. Employment law exists for a reason. Workers are entitled to a minimum amount of statutory paid annual leave because periods of rest and leisure are critical to their mental and physical health. The increased morale, creativity and productivity which are cited as the desired results of the unlimited leave policy can all exist independently of worker well-being. I remain doubtful, therefore, as to whether being 'able to take as much holiday as they want' is either the true intention or the probable outcome of this policy.

31   What does the writer imply about the founder of the multinational corporation?

    A   He is unwise to employ his daughter in his company.
    B   He is dishonestly copying an idea from another company.
    C   He is using his daughter to make a planned change appear more acceptable.
    D   He is merely trying to increase his personal popularity.

32   Which phrase could correctly replace 'Setting aside' in line 5?

    A   As an example of
    B   Because we accept
    C   If we ignore for now
    D   Taking as a starting point

33   The writer compares the multinational corporation and the internet company in order to demonstrate that

    A   unlimited leave is more likely to work in a more diverse company.
    B   employees in a smaller company have more loyalty to each other.
    C   it is difficult for workers to assess what is best for their company.
    D   what works in one company may be unsuitable for another.

34   What does the writer state about the unlimited leave policy in the third paragraph?

    A   It increases the employees' workloads.
    B   It sets unreasonable criteria to consider before leave can be taken.
    C   It could harm the employees' careers in the long term.
    D   It makes them feel under an obligation to take leave at inappropriate times.

35   What generalisation does the writer make about office workers in the fourth paragraph?

    A   They can often be unaware of their legal rights.
    B   They can have a strong influence on each other's behaviour.
    C   They tend to be more productive when there is a promotion on offer.
    D   They prefer to have fixed guidelines regarding terms and conditions.

36   In the last paragraph, the writer questions whether

    A   it was really the staff at the internet company who had the idea for an unlimited leave policy.
    B   employees can be trusted to keep track of their working hours.
    C   abolishing a fixed work timetable actually gives workers more freedom.
    D   it is time to update the employment laws relating to paid leave.

Part 6

You are going to read four reviews of a book about memory called *Pieces of Light*. For questions
37–40, choose from the reviewers **A–D**. The reviewers may be chosen more than once.
Mark your answers **on the separate answer sheet**.

Reviews of *Pieces of Light*

Four reviewers give their opinions on a book about memory by Charles Fernyhough

A   In my view, the most important message of *Pieces of Light* is that the 'reconstructive nature of memory
can make it unreliable'. It is wrong to see memories as fixed biochemical or electrical traces in the brain,
like books in a giant library that you could access if only you knew how. People are becoming increasingly
aware that memory is, in fact, unstable. The stories in *Pieces of Light* may persuade a few more – and
anyone who reads them will enjoy Fernyhough's effortless prose. He returns repeatedly to his central
message using a sophisticated and engaging blend of findings from science, ideas from literature and
examples from personal narratives. Yet in disabusing us of our misconceptions, and despite this being the
stated aim of the book, Fernyhough leaves us with little sense of a scientific explanation to put in their place.

B   'Remembering is a serious business,' Charles Fernyhough warns. It is this respect for his subject that makes
Pieces of Light such an immense pleasure, as Fernyhough sees the emerging science of memory through
the lens of his own recollections. In the hands of a lesser writer, such reliance on personal experience could
rapidly descend into self-indulgence and cliché, but Fernyhough – a psychologist and published novelist –
remains restrained and lyrical throughout. As Fernyhough examines the way the brain continually rewrites
our past, it is almost impossible not to question the accuracy of our recollections. Even the events that
we recall with the most vivid sensory detail are not to be trusted, he maintains. Although I remain to be
persuaded, Fernyhough does serve up the latest findings in neuroscience and quotes academic studies
without ever baffling the reader along the way.

C   Fernyhough, who is a popular science writer as well as an academic psychologist, wrote this book because
he is worried that too many people still think of memory in terms of a vast personal DVD library. He sets
out to show the reader how he believes it to actually operate, and I for one was convinced. The author
plays a key role in his own book, returning to places that were very familiar to him in childhood to see how
much he can remember. However, he gets hopelessly lost. Though Fernyhough is a gifted writer who can
turn any experience into lively prose, these autobiographical passages are the least successful of *Pieces
of Light* because they are too disconnected from any scientific insights about memory. There are also
frequent references to literature. Yet whereas others might find these a distraction from the main narrative,
I personally found the balance between science and literature refreshing and well judged.

D   A major theme of Charles Fernyhough's book is that remembering is less a matter of encoding, storing and
retrieving an accurate record of events, and more a matter of adjusting memories to current circumstances,
which may then alter them for future recollection. He mixes the latest findings in neuroscience with
in-depth case histories. Nor is Fernyhough uncomfortable using personal testimony to put warm flesh on
hard science: sizeable sections of the book are taken up with him exploring his own past. These do not
add greatly to the book, and it is hard for the reader not to wonder whether it is really worth the effort of
ploughing on with him. This weariness is reflected in his writing style. Surprisingly, however, Fernyhough is a
lucid, concise and knowledgeable guide to all the data that generally stay buried deep in specialist journals,
and that is where the book really springs to life.

Which reviewer

expresses a similar opinion to B on how clearly the science is presented?

37

has a different opinion to all the others on the quality of the writing?

38

shares C's view of how well the writer brings together diverse academic disciplines?

39

has a similar view to D on the effectiveness of the writer's emphasis on his personal memories?

40

Part 7

You are going to read a newspaper article about a project at a natural history museum. Six paragraphs have been removed from the article. Choose from the paragraphs **A–G** the one which fits each gap (**41–46**). There is one extra paragraph which you do not need to use.
Mark your answers **on the separate answer sheet**.

Taking Dinosaurs Apart

Pulling apart limbs, sawing through ribs and separating skull bones are activities usually associated with surgeons rather than museum staff. However, that is exactly what is going on at the Smithsonian's National Museum of Natural History in Washington DC, USA. Renovations to the museum's dinosaur hall, which started recently, have necessitated the dismantling and removal of its collection of dinosaur and extinct mammal skeletons, some of which weigh as much as five tons.

> **41**

One particular specimen which curator Matthew Carrano can't wait to get hold of is a meat-eating Jurassic dinosaur called Allosaurus, which has been on display for 30 years. 'Scientifically, this particular Allosaurus is well known,' he explains, because 'for a long time, it was one of the only Allosaurus specimens that represented a single individual animal.'

> **42**

The Smithsonian's five-meter-long Allosaurus, however, is definitely one, unique individual. So once the crystallized glue holding it together is removed, researchers and conservators can get a better sense of how the creature's joints actually fitted together in life.

> **43**

Another modification the museum plans to make to its Allosaurus is removing a couple of centimeters from its tail, which is not original fossil but casts of vertebrae. 'The tail on the Smithsonian's specimen is too long,' says Peter May, owner and president of the company in charge of dismantling, conserving, and remounting the 58 specimens in the museum's dinosaur hall. He explains that the skeleton on display has over 50 vertebrae, when it should have something closer to 45.

> **44**

Slicing a thin cross-section out of a leg or rib bone can help with that. By placing a slice under a microscope, researchers will be able to count growth rings on the bone, the number of which would have increased throughout the creature's life, very much like the rings on a cross-section of a tree trunk.

> **45**

One example which Carrano wishes to investigate further is an apparent blow to the Allosaurus's left side. 'The shoulder blade looks like it has healed improperly,' he explains. If the damaged shoulder blade can be fitted together with the ribs which are held in storage, paleontologists might be able to determine the severity and cause of the damage.

Finally, Carrano hopes to be able to compare the Allosaurus with another dinosaur in the collection called Labrosaurus. Labrosaurus is known only from a single bone – a lower jaw with a distortion which is believed to have been caused by disease or injury. 'The two front teeth are missing and there's an abscess there,' Carrano explains.

> **46**

But in order to confirm their suspicion, Carrano and his colleagues will have to wait a while. 'A lot of what we hope to learn won't be accessible to us until the exhibits have been taken down and we can have a good look at them,' he says. So he won't be able to get his hands on the Allosaurus quite yet.

A Dismantling the Allosaurus and removing the plaster and glue covering it can also reveal whether the animal suffered any injuries when alive.

B The Smithsonian's team should be able to take it apart in large chunks in a single day, but even once they've dismantled it they'll still have hours of work ahead of them, breaking the skeleton down further into individual bones and cleaning them.

C These endeavors will modernize a space which has never seen a major overhaul. It will also give researchers a chance to make detailed studies of the exhibits – some of which haven't been touched in decades.

D There are also plans to slim it down a little. When the museum first displayed the Allosaurus, preparators decided to use plaster casts of the ribs instead of the actual specimens, which resulted in a heavier-looking skeleton. Curators hope that the final, remounted skeleton will more closely resemble the dinosaur's natural shape.

E However, this dinosaur, previously classified as a separate species is now thought to be a type of Allosaurus. Both of the specimens come from the same quarry, and what's more the Allosaurus is missing the exact same bone, so it's entirely possible that it actually belongs to the Smithsonian Allosaurus.

F In addition to correcting mistakes such as this, made when the specimens were first displayed, Carrano would also like to determine the age of the Allosaurus.

G There are Allosaurus skeletons in museum collections across the world, but most consist of bones from a number of different examples of the species. This has made it difficult for scientists to work out how the entire skeleton fits together.

Part 8

You are going to read an article in which four academics give their views on fiction. For questions **47–56**, choose from the academics (**A–D**). The academics may be chosen more than once.

Mark your answers **on the separate answer sheet**.

Which academic

compares books to other story-telling art forms?	47
admits to gaps in their literary knowledge?	48
suggests a possible consequence of not reading novels?	49
points out that opinion about a book depends on the period in which it is being judged?	50
explains why readers sometimes choose to read books which are not considered classic works of literature?	51
believes that it is possible to improve any novel?	52
gives reassurance about people whose choice of reading is limited?	53
says that no-one should feel obliged to read a particular type of book?	54
gives another writer's opinion on why people enjoy reading literature?	55
defends their right to judge particular types of novels?	56

Why Do We Read Novels?

We asked a group of academics for their views on the appeal of fiction

A   Cathy Smith

Is a work by a prize-winning novelist better than a trashy summer blockbuster? Undoubtedly, if you're looking for a literary masterpiece. But it's not 'better' if you're simply looking for escapism. 'Literary fiction', unlike 'genre fiction' such as mystery or romance, is not about escaping from reality. Instead it provides a means to better understand the world. What makes a work deserve the title of literary fiction can be pinned down, to a certain extent, by critical analysis of the writer's techniques. Yet a huge element of the appeal of literary fiction lies in something almost indefinable – the brilliant, original idea; the insight that, once written down, seems the only way to say something. Writers of fiction have to recruit or seduce us into their world – only then do we trust them to take us on a journey with them. The books we put down after only a few pages are those which have failed to make that connection with us.

B   Matteo Bianco

A novel – whether for adults or children – takes you places, emotionally and imaginatively, which you would never otherwise have visited. However, I don't think you should put yourself under any more pressure to finish 'a classic' than a kids' comic. And if by 'classics' we mean Tolstoy, Proust, Hardy and so on, then my own reading is distinctly patchy. The author Martin Amis once said that the only way we have of evaluating the quality of a book is whether it retains a readership. I think that's fair enough, though it's imprecise. A work of fiction can always be fine-tuned in such a way that the final experience for the reader is enhanced, and this fact must say something about the theoretical (if not practical) possibility of stating that one book is better than another. And while I can't prove that a single copy of a classic work of fiction is a greater gift to the world than a million trashy romances, I'm going to go ahead and say it's so anyway.

C   Gita Sarka

The author Albert Camus says that the appeal of narrative art lies in its power to organise life in such a way that we can reflect on it from a distance and experience it anew. Distinct from television or film, literature allows us significant control over our experience of what's being presented to us. One book I would always tell anyone to read is *The Life and Times of Michael K* – a literary prize winner, but hated by some of my colleagues. It's a classic for me because of what it says about living in difficult times; to a lot of people it's just a bit boring and the main character doesn't speak enough. Categories such as 'literary masterpieces' and even 'literature' do not exist independently of their assessors – assessors who are bound in an era and see value in part through the eyes of that era. Personally, I find it impossible to make claims that one work is better than another. I can say why it might be worthwhile to study it, but that's all.

D   George C. Schwarz

If, at a certain time in their life a person is interested in just one particular genre or author, that's fine as long as they have the opportunity of reading a wide range of books throughout their lives. These opportunities can come through family members, teachers and friends who can create the reading landscape and encourage them to look wider and further. A famous writer once said that it's easy to recognise the people who don't read fiction, as their outlook on life is narrower and less imaginative, and they find it hard to put themselves in other people's shoes. It's a generalisation, but with elements of truth. The power of fiction begins with fairy tales, nursery rhymes and picture books, which give children ways of looking at the world outside their own experience. Literature teachers often recommend reading 'the classics'. But what classics, whose and which era? In a way it doesn't matter – the key point is that one can't escape from a need for shared references and reading experience.

WRITING (1 hour 30 minutes)

Part 1

You **must** answer this question. Write your answer in **220–260** words in an appropriate style.

---

1   Your class has watched a TV programme on ways of keeping the urban environment clean and tidy. You have made the notes below:

> **Ways of keeping the urban environment clean and tidy:**
> * legislation
> * public awareness campaigns
> * public services

> Some opinions expressed in the programme:
>
> "Laws against polluting should be tougher."
>
> "The media need to encourage people to act responsibly."
>
> "The government needs to spend more on keeping our cities clean."

Write an essay for your tutor discussing **two** of the ways in your notes. You should **explain which way of keeping the urban environment clean and tidy is more important** and **provide reasons** to support your opinion.

You may, if you wish, make use of the opinions expressed in the programme, but you should use your own words as far as possible.

Part 2

Write an answer to **one** of the questions **2–4** in this part. Write your answer in **220–260** words in an appropriate style.

---

2   You receive this letter from a Canadian friend.

> …
>
> I'm doing a project on the use of technology in education around the world. Could you tell me about your experience of using technology for learning? What do you think are the main advantages and disadvantages of using technology for learning?
>
> I look forward to hearing from you.

Write your **letter** in reply. You do not need to include postal addresses.

3   The company you work for is planning to improve the staff canteen. You have conducted a survey among employees to find out what they would like. Your manager has asked you to write a report in which you describe how you conducted your survey, explain what you discovered and recommend what you think your company should provide.

Write your **report**.

4   You regularly look at a website that is devoted to reviewing films. You feel that it does not contain enough reviews of films produced in your country. Write a review of a film from your country, commenting on whether you feel it is typical of films from your country and explaining why you think it would be of interest to an international audience.

Write your **review**.

LISTENING (approximately 40 minutes)

Part 1

You will hear three different extracts.

For questions **1–6**, choose the answer (**A**, **B** or **C**) which fits best according to what you hear. There are two questions for each extract.

Extract One

You hear two friends talking about online privacy.

1 Why does the man mention his uncle?

    A to criticise his attitude to technology

    B to challenge a recommendation made by the woman

    C to illustrate the power of the media

2 They agree that modern technology

    A makes little difference to the accessibility of personal information.

    B is less invasive than some people suggest.

    C will continue to reduce people's privacy.

Extract Two

You hear two trainee chefs discussing the issue of food waste.

3 What does the woman think about her boss's ideas?

    A She's surprised at his forward-looking attitude.

    B She's dismissive of his attention to detail.

    C She's concerned about his generosity towards customers.

4 In reacting to the woman's comments, the man reveals that he is

    A determined to change practices at his own workplace.

    B unsure about the facts she is presenting to him.

    C doubtful whether his chef would accept new ideas.

Extract Three

You hear two students talking about an experiment into the way people perceive time.

5   The woman thinks the experiment was important because

    A it provided unexpected results.

    B it presented a great physical challenge.

    C it raised public awareness of the subject.

6   She believes celebrating special events

    A convinces people that time passes more quickly.

    B provides people with pleasant memories.

    C gives people a sense of structure when recalling the past.

Part 2

You will hear a woman called Sarah Harvey talking about her work with an environmental organisation which helps to protect the seas from pollution. For questions **7–14**, complete the sentences with a word or short phrase.

Protecting the Seas from Pollution

The organisation Sarah works for is called **(7)** ....

Sarah was surprised to learn that seabirds have been known to eat

(8) .... on occasions.

Sarah says that plastic can be compared to a **(9)** ....

because of the way it absorbs dangerous substances.

Sarah learned that the toxins in plastic harm the **(10)** ....

system of many creatures.

Sarah explains how the breakdown of plastic items into small particles is caused by

(11) .... and the effects of the sun.

Sarah says that most plastic in the sea has its origin in **(12)** .... sources.

Sarah gives the example of **(13)** .... as something to use

instead of household detergents.

Sarah strongly advises car owners to prevent **(14)** .... from their vehicles.

Part 3

You will hear a radio interview in which two web designers called Rob Thorn and Sophie Unwin are discussing aspects of their work. For questions **15–20**, choose the answer (**A, B, C** or **D**) which fits best according to what you hear.

15 Sophie says that the work of web designers
    A   must reflect constant evolution in the field.
    B   is subject to rigid time constraints.
    C   should prioritise aesthetic considerations.
    D   is limited by technical requirements.

16 Sophie believes the success of a website depends on
    A   the originality of its appearance.
    B   the balance of text and illustration.
    C   the emphasis on pictorial accuracy.
    D   the logical organisation of its content.

17 Why did Rob first turn his attention to website design?
    A   It offered an exciting new challenge.
    B   It was an outlet for his training in graphic art.
    C   He discovered it was a good way to make money.
    D   He found he had a particular talent for gaming.

18 The change from being a freelancer to working for a company has led Sophie to feel
    A   relieved she carries less responsibility.
    B   sorry she has work that is less predictable.
    C   disappointed she has less contact with clients.
    D   pleased she spends less time on administration.

19 What is Rob's strategy when dealing with clients?
    A   to defend his own ideas vigorously
    B   to overstate the time a project will take
    C   to conduct meetings in a formal atmosphere
    D   to focus on discussing financial details

20 Both Rob and Sophie say they find inspiration by
    A   developing a heightened perception of everyday things.
    B   appreciating new technological developments.
    C   studying the work of other designers.
    D   experimenting with other art forms.

Part 4

You will hear five short extracts in which people are talking about spending time working on a magazine.

TASK ONE

For questions **21–25**, choose from the list (**A–H**) the benefit each speaker gained from the experience of working on a magazine.

TASK TWO

For questions **26–30**, choose from the list (**A–H**) the personal quality each speaker thinks is most important for magazine work.

While you listen, you must complete both tasks.

A	increased confidence	
B	improved IT skills	
C	ideas for a future career	Speaker 1 ☐ 21
D	useful contacts	Speaker 2 ☐ 22
E	pride in an achievement	Speaker 3 ☐ 23
F	the ability to work with colleagues	Speaker 4 ☐ 24
G	broader knowledge of the industry	Speaker 5 ☐ 25
H	greater self-awareness	

A	the ability to get on with people	
B	an attention to detail	
C	the ability to concentrate	Speaker 1 ☐ 26
D	a single-minded determination	Speaker 2 ☐ 27
E	formal qualifications	Speaker 3 ☐ 28
F	good organisational skills	Speaker 4 ☐ 29
G	innovative thinking	Speaker 5 ☐ 30
H	willingness to work long hours	

SPEAKING (15 minutes)

There are two examiners. One (the interlocutor) conducts the test, providing you with the necessary materials and explaining what you have to do. The other examiner (the assessor) is introduced to you, but then takes no further part in the interaction.

Part 1 (2 minutes)

The interlocutor first asks you and your partner for some information about yourselves, then widens the scope of the questions by asking about e.g. your leisure activities, studies, travel and daily life. You are expected to respond to the interlocutor's questions and listen to what your partner has to say.

Part 2 (a one-minute 'long turn' for each candidate, plus a 30-second response from the second candidate)

You are each given the opportunity to talk for about a minute, and to comment briefly after your partner has spoken.

The interlocutor gives you a set of three pictures and asks you to talk about two of them for about one minute. It is important to listen carefully to the interlocutor's instructions. The interlocutor then asks your partner a question about your pictures and your partner responds briefly.

You are then given another set of pictures to look at. Your partner talks about these pictures for about one minute. This time the interlocutor asks you a question about your partner's pictures and you respond briefly.

Part 3 (4 minutes)

In this part of the test, you and your partner are asked to talk together. The interlocutor places a question and some text prompts on the table between you. This stimulus provides the basis for a discussion, after which you will need to make a decision on the topic in question. The interlocutor explains what you have to do.

Part 4 (5 minutes)

The interlocutor asks some further questions, which leads to a more general discussion of the topic you have discussed in Part 3. You may comment on your partner's answers if you wish.

Test 8

READING AND USE OF ENGLISH (1 hour 30 minutes)

Part 1

For questions **1–8**, read the text below and decide which answer (**A, B, C** or **D**) best fits each gap. There is an example at the beginning (**0**).

Mark your answers **on the separate answer sheet**.

Example:

0 A borne   **B** endeavoured   **C** undertaken   **D** committed

0	A	B	C	D
	—	—	▬	—

Citizen Science

'Citizen Science' is a new term given to scientific research which is **(0)** …….. by members of the public, working in **(1)** …….. with professional scientists and scientific institutions. The type of research involved ranges from fairly passive activities, such as downloading software which allows your home computer to analyse scientific data, to more active research such as recording **(2)** …….. of endangered species in your local area.

The term 'Citizen Science' may be relatively recent, but the **(3)** …….. is centuries old. Amateur scientists, particularly naturalists, have contributed to science for hundreds of years. However, the internet has **(4)** …….. changed the way in which enthusiasts can work together and share their findings. One example of this is 'Galaxy Zoo', which **(5)** …….. on volunteers to classify galaxies online. Within the first seven months of the project, volunteers had analysed 900,000 galaxies – a rate of analysis that would **(6)** …….. have been unachievable.

In addition to aiding researchers, citizen science projects also **(7)** …….. an educational purpose, encouraging more people to become actively **(8)** …….. in science.

1   **A** unity   **B** participation   **C** accordance   **D** collaboration

2   **A** sightings   **B** visions   **C** detections   **D** looks

3   **A** operation   **B** practice   **C** manner   **D** routine

4   **A** fundamentally **B** centrally   **C** principally **D** primarily

5   **A** brought   **B** sent   **C** turned   **D** called

6   **A** anyhow   **B** hence   **C** otherwise   **D** thereby

7   **A** present   **B** serve   **C** deliver   **D** assist

8   **A** absorbed   **B** consumed   **C** dedicated   **D** engaged

Part 2

For questions **9–16**, read the text below and think of the word which best fits each gap. Use only **one** word in each gap. There is an example at the beginning (**0**).

Write your answers **IN CAPITAL LETTERS on the separate answer sheet**.

Example: | **0** | | *O* | N | | | | | | | | | | | | | | | | | |

Walking – the Best Exercise

Exercise researchers at Edinburgh University have discovered that British people walk **(0)** .... average 120km less per year than they **(9)** .... just a decade ago. Experts recommend that people should walk **(10)** .... 10,000 and 12,000 steps a day to stay healthy, but if their figures **(11)** .... to be believed, the **(12)** .... of British people only manage 3,000. Naturally, this concerns the researchers, who point out the wide range of physical and mental health benefits to people of all ages.

For people who want to take things **(13)** .... stage further and use walking as a keep-fit activity, much information is now available online on walking technique; and new exercise concepts like 'speed walking' and 'power walking' have become popular. According to these sources, it is important to relax the shoulders and keep them down, to swing the arms in time **(14)** .... the stride and to lean forward slightly from the ankles. Also, in **(15)** .... to increase walking speed, it is advised to concentrate on frequency of steps made as opposed **(16)** .... length of stride.

Part 3

For questions **17–24**, read the text below. Use the word given in capitals at the end of some of the lines to form a word that fits in the gap **in the same line**. There is an example at the beginning (**0**).

Write your answers **IN CAPITAL LETTERS on the separate answer sheet**.

Example:

0	A	R	C	H	I	T	E	C	T	U	R	A	L					

Living with Skyscrapers

Skyscrapers are **(0)** …….. wonders of modern cities. There is an   **ARCHITECT**

increasing **(17)** …….. on them to maximise city space and tourists   **RELY**

love to admire them. But while tall buildings look **(18)** …….. from afar,   **AWE**

in many ways their most **(19)** …….. impact is at ground level.   **SIGNIFY**

Wind speed increases in **(20)** …….. to height, and tall buildings force   **RELATE**

winds that would normally stay well above street level groundwards.

This creates micro-climates at the foot of the building that feel

(21) …….. colder than surrounding areas. Skyscrapers also cast   **CONSIDER**

(22) …….. shadows. In hot climates this is appreciated, but in colder   **SUBSTANCE**

countries, where the sun is welcomed, it's more likely to be a cause

of **(23)** …….. . Groups of tall buildings also affect the transmission   **ANNOY**

of sound at ground level and can result in noise being amplified to

intolerable levels.

Some architects have been accused of being **(24)** …….. of the impact   **DISMISS**

of skyscrapers on pedestrians' lives and of disregarding the fact

that, in order to encourage walking and street life, buildings need to

interact with what is at their base.

Part 4

For questions **25–30**, complete the second sentence so that it has a similar meaning to the first sentence, using the word given. **Do not change the word given.** You must use between **three** and **six** words, including the word given. Here is an example (**0**).

Example:

0 James would only speak to the head of department alone.

   ON

   James ………………………………… to the head of department alone.

The gap can be filled with the words 'insisted on speaking', so you write:

Example: | **0** | INSISTED ON SPEAKING |

Write **only** the missing words **IN CAPITAL LETTERS on the separate answer sheet**.

___

25 It's none of your business what I choose to do in my free time.

   NOTHING

   What I choose to do in my free time …………………………….... with you.

26 We will let you know if your travel itinerary needs to be changed in any way.

   NOTIFY

   We will …………………………….... that need to be made to your travel itinerary.

27 There was no need for us to rush to the station as our train was delayed.

   TAKEN

   We could …………………………….... getting to the station as our train was delayed.

28 David reduced the amount of chocolate he ate, because his doctor advised him to.

   ADVICE

   As a result of ………………………….…... down on the amount of chocolate he ate.

29 That was the most stimulating lecture on climate change that I've ever heard.

   MORE

   I've yet ………………………….…... stimulating lecture on climate change.

30 As soon as the company advertised the job vacancy, the applications came flooding in.

   HAD

   No ………………………….…... advertised, than the applications came flooding in.

Part 5

You are going to read a magazine article about light pollution. For questions **31–36**, choose the answer (**A, B, C** or **D**) which you think fits best according to the text.

Mark your answers **on the separate answer sheet**.

Our Vanishing Night

If humans were truly at home under the light of the moon and stars, we would go in darkness happily, the midnight world as visible to us as it is to the vast number of nocturnal species on this planet who feel at home in it. Instead, we are diurnal creatures, with eyes adapted to living in the sun's light. This basic fact is engrained deep in our genetic make-up, even though most of us don't think of ourselves as diurnal beings any more than we think of ourselves as primates or mammals or Earthlings. Yet it's the only way to explain what we've done to the night.

We've somehow managed to engineer the night to receive us by filling it with light. This kind of control is no different from the feat of damming a river. Its benefits come with consequences – called light pollution – whose effects scientists are only now beginning to study. Light pollution is largely the result of bad lighting design, which allows artificial light to shine outward and upward into the sky, where it's not wanted, instead of focusing it downward, where it is. Ill-designed lighting washes out the darkness of night, altering light levels and light rhythms to which many forms of life, including ourselves, have adapted. Wherever man-made light spills into the natural world, some aspects of life – migration, reproduction, feeding – is affected.

For most human history, the phrase 'light pollution' would have made no sense. Imagine walking towards London on a moonlit night around 1800, when it was Earth's most populous city. Nearly a million people lived there, making do, as they always had, with candles, torches and lanterns. Only a few houses were lit by gas, and there would be no public gaslights in the streets or squares for another seven years. From a few miles away, you would have been more likely to smell London than to see its dim collective glow.

We've lit up the night as if it were an unoccupied country, when nothing could be further from the truth. Among mammals alone, the number of nocturnal species is astonishing. Light is a powerful biological force, and on many species it acts as a magnet attracting them to it. The effect is so powerful that scientists speak of songbirds and seabirds being 'captured' by searchlights on land or by the light from gas flares on marine oil platforms, circling and circling in the thousands until they drop. Migrating at night, birds are apt to collide with brightly lit tall buildings; immature birds on their first journey suffer disproportionately. Some birds – blackbirds and nightingales, among others – sing at unnatural hours in the presence of artificial light.

line 29 It was once thought that light pollution only affected astronomers, who need to see the night sky in all its glorious clarity. Unlike astronomers, most of us may not need an undiminished view of the night sky for our work, but like most other creatures we do need darkness. Denying darkness is futile. It is as essential to maintaining our biological welfare as light itself; the price of modifying our internal clockwork means it doesn't operate as it should, causing various physical ailments. The regular oscillation of waking and sleep in our lives is nothing less than a biological expression of the regular oscillation of light on Earth. So fundamental are these rhythms to our being that messing with them is akin to altering our center of gravity.

In the end, humans are no less trapped by light pollution than the frogs in a pond near a brightly lit highway. Living in a glare of our own making, we have cut ourselves off from our evolutionary and cultural heritage – the light of the stars and the rhythms of day and night. In a very real sense, light pollution causes us to lose sight of our true place in the universe, to forget the scale of our being, which is best measured against the dimensions of a deep night with the Milky Way – the edge of our galaxy – arching overhead.

31 In the first paragraph, what does the writer suggest about darkness?

    A It is linked to our survival instinct.

    B Early humans became accustomed to it.

    C We are one of the few animals who fear it.

    D Our response to it is intrinsic to our species.

32 The writer refers to damming a river to underline the fact that

    A beneficial modifications can have negative effects.

    B water and light are equally crucial to human and animal life.

    C light pollution might have a variety of sources.

    D it's inadvisable to interfere with key environmental features.

33 What point is the writer making about London in 1800?

    A It was virtually invisible at night.

    B It was famed for its resourceful lighting.

    C Its inhabitants were subject to strict laws regarding lighting.

    D Its lack of illumination made it a dangerous place.

34 In the fourth paragraph, the writer suggests that light pollution has caused some animals to

    A develop physiological adaptations to brighter conditions.

    B alter behavioural patterns.

    C risk becoming endangered species.

    D be more susceptible to predation.

35 In the fifth paragraph, the writer draws a comparison between 'denying darkness' (line 29) and

    A maintaining our biological welfare.

    B modifying our internal clockwork.

    C causing various physical ailments.

    D altering our centre of gravity.

36 The overall tone of the article is one of

    A concern about how escalating light pollution will affect species in the future.

    B regret at the loss of a fundamental aspect of our relationship with nature.

    C optimism about our increasing awareness of a key environmental issue.

    D doubt as to whether the effects of light pollution can ever be reversed.

Part 6

You are going to read four extracts from articles in which scientists give their views on zoos. For questions **37–40**, choose from the scientists **A–D**. The scientists may be chosen more than once. Mark your answers **on the separate answer sheet**.

The Role of Zoos

A I'm very well aware of the downsides of maintaining wild animals in captivity, but the fact that they're far from ideal for the particular specimens which are unfortunate enough to be held captive doesn't mean that zoos can't help wildlife in general. Those who would like them all to close should remember that many people can't afford to go and see animals in their natural habitat. I condemn completely the practice of having animals such as dolphins and monkeys put on shows for visitors, but having one of the zoo keepers give a short talk on an animal while children look at it is an excellent way of teaching them about wildlife. Furthermore, zoos, particularly the bigger, more famous ones, have become leaders in projects such as the reintroduction of captive-born animals to the wild, which are boosting efforts to save those threatened with extinction.

B Having worked in many different zoos over the years, I have developed something of an ambivalent attitude towards them. Zoos have always been in the entertainment business, and as long as the animals are not suffering, and the tricks they are asked to carry out are activities they would do naturally, that's fine. This doesn't mean, however, that I like seeing animals in cages. Animals in zoos are plagued with mental and behavioural problems which lead to a drastically shortened life expectancy. Far more could be done to improve their quality of life, but unfortunately, many boards and directors see their zoos as a community resource similar to the local pool or library, and fail to consider the needs of the animals when it comes to allocating budgets.

C The work that zoos do on a global level to co-ordinate population management of endangered species has made a real difference. One notable success in this area is the case of the Californian condor, for instance. Having said that, I still question whether we should be keeping animals in zoos at all. In recent decades, huge sums have been spent on improving the habitats of animals at many zoos, but ultimately we have to accept that an enclosure, however stimulating, isn't the right place for a wild creature. If we have to keep animals in captivity, then surely safari parks, in which the humans are enclosed in vehicles, while the animals roam free, are a better alternative. Additionally, by setting wildlife in a more natural environment, they provide real opportunities for visitors to develop their understanding of the animals, which is a claim I have never believed when it's made by zoos.

D I imagine that many of the strongest critics of zoos rarely set foot in one, but I would urge them to take another look. Entry charges are high, but when you look at the first-class facilities for both visitors and animals, you can see that the money is being used wisely. Zoo animals across the globe now live in conditions which closely resemble their natural habitat and allow them to behave in as natural a way as possible. It's unfortunate that, despite making these changes, some zoos have chosen to continue the practice of having animals perform for the crowds. These distasteful displays have no place in modern society. The emphasis now needs to be firmly on the well-being of animals – not just those in zoos, but also those whose continued existence in the wild is in question. This is an area where zoos could do much more to make use of their considerable expertise.

Which scientist

has a different opinion from A on whether traditional zoos serve an educational purpose?

37

has the same opinion as A on using zoo animals as a form of entertainment?

38

shares an opinion with A on the contribution that zoos make to conservation?

39

has a different opinion from D on the financial choices which zoo managers make?

40

Part 7

You are going to read a magazine article about geothermal power in Iceland. Six paragraphs have been removed from the article. Choose from the paragraphs **A–G** the one which fits each gap **(41–46)**. There is one extra paragraph which you do not need to use.

Mark your answers **on the separate answer sheet**.

Geothermal Power in Iceland

Iceland makes use of geothermal power, where heat from the centre of the earth causes water below the surface to become superheated in the form of hot springs or geysers

Around 24 million years ago, Iceland first rose from the ocean as a collective of lava and gas-spewing volcanoes. Perched atop the rift between divergent North American and Eurasian tectonic plates, this island of fire and ice is still shaped by powerful subterranean forces. Eruptions, mud pools and spouting geysers are all part of daily Icelandic life.

41

Fast forward in time, and geothermal resources now produce 25% of Iceland's electrical power, as well as meeting the country's heating and hot water needs. On the face of it, Iceland appears to be sitting pretty with regard to renewable energy supplies. However, the country's geothermal resources aren't quite as clean, green or limitless as you might imagine. Studies have shown that the overuse of geothermal resources degrades water reserves permanently, or for significant lengths of time. According to energy consultant Ketill Sigurjonsson, there is an ongoing debate about just how sustainable Iceland's geothermal resources are. 'If energy companies can't find a way to stabilise the national power output, then this may create severe difficulties for them further down the line,' he explains.

42

Much of this is directed at the government's policy several years back of selling vast quantities of energy to metal-producing companies and approving construction of several smelters – the machines used to extract metals from ores. When Iceland's oldest smelter started production more than four decades ago, the country's metal industry accounted for no more than 3% of its Gross Domestic Product.

43

The smelters now consume about 75% of all electricity generated in Iceland. The contracts the government negotiated with the metal companies mean they pay relatively little for the energy they consume. Measures are therefore being taken to reduce Iceland's dependence on metal production, with the government trying to attract other large-scale end users of electrical power.

44

'The Icelandic government and geothermal energy companies are now pushing again for the exploitation of Iceland's geothermal resources to serve industry,' says Miriam Rose, a geologist at Reykjavik-based NGO Saving Iceland. 'However, there's increasing evidence that their estimates of available energy are overstated, and there are also serious pollution considerations. Many Icelanders are very worried about this, especially as the springs and geysers are a major tourist attraction.

45

According to the US Environmental Protection Agency, geothermal sites release around five percent of the carbon dioxide, one percent of the sulphur dioxide, and less than one percent of the nitrous oxide that's emitted by a coal-fired site of an equal size. But crucially, Reykjavik Energy's Hellisheidi and Nesjavellir geothermal plants currently emit around 28,000 tonnes of hydrogen sulphide annually. A recent study linked emissions of this gas with the increased incidence of asthma among Reykjavik's residents, and strict new government regulations established in 2010 have forced the geothermal industry to slash hydrogen sulphide emissions from its plants or face closure.

46

Perhaps the biggest shake-up in the Icelandic geothermal industry will take place if 'IceLink' – a 1,000 kilometre undersea power cable connecting the Icelandic and British grids – gets the go-ahead. Still in the conceptual stage, it would be the longest undersea cable in the world, costing around US$6.6 billion and taking four years to build.

A However, not everyone is convinced that this is the way forward. Experts maintain that compared to the geological time scale of oil regeneration, geothermal energy is relatively renewable.

B In less than a decade, these new plants were producing 870,000 tonnes annually, virtually all destined for overseas markets. Soon, such exports were eclipsing fisheries exports in value for the first time in the island's history.

C Not only that, but Iceland's geothermal power sector as a whole is likely to incur public criticism. Given that the industry has already drawn some negative publicity, it could do without further condemnation.

D Geothermal resources may be renewable if used sustainably, but they aren't emissions free, as locals and visitors who walk the streets of Iceland's capital can testify. However, emissions rates associated with geothermal power plants are much lower than emissions from coal or natural gas-fired power plants.

E Given the vast amounts of energy flowing just below the ground, it's little wonder that Iceland is now pushing the boundaries of geothermal technology and resource use. While naturally hot water has long been harnessed by Iceland's inhabitants, it wasn't until the oil and gas price hikes of the 1970s that the island began to use it to produce electricity.

F Acting on these requirements, experiments and projects are underway at various sites to ensure that the situation is brought under control. It should soon be clear how successful they've been.

G It was recently announced, for example, that the national power company had signed an agreement to supply power to a new silicon production plant being constructed in Helguvik on Iceland's southwest coast. Ecologists, however, have renewed their concerns.

Part 8

You are going to read an article about polyglots, people who speak many languages. For questions **47–56**, choose from the people (**A–D**). The people may be chosen more than once.

Mark your answers **on the separate answer sheet**.

Which person mentions

a lack of concern about their identity?	47
advice about when to fit in an important aspect of language acquisition?	48
a reason for concentrating on one language at a time?	49
a means of coping with the most challenging phase of language acquisition?	50
a description of the stages in a person's language learning method?	51
an early appreciation of an advantage of being multilingual?	52
a long-term view of their own language learning?	53
an emotion brought on by the sound of a language?	54
appreciation for an experience arising from being a polyglot?	55
the prospect of changing their language-learning goal?	56

Natural Born Linguists

What drives multi-language speakers? Martin Williams finds out.

A Ludmila Orlova

Being multilingual is fundamental to who I am because I think in different languages. My mind starts a thought in one language, then finds a particular word in another language that fits exactly what I am thinking. Each language resonates with me in a distinct way. Russian makes me more melancholic because of its minor tone, for example. There's a downside, though: when I'm in a monolingual environment for too long, I yearn to switch to a different language. I have to think 'will this person understand me if I say something in language X?' I had an early start at learning languages. I moved to the US from the former Soviet Union when I was three and learnt English quickly. For some reason though, my primary teacher didn't think I was bright enough to study languages at secondary school, which just goes to show you that general academic achievement isn't always a good indicator of one's ability to learn a language. If I had studied languages the formal way in school, I would never have become a polyglot.

B Simon Richards

I was always fascinated by languages and accents – I tried to mimic them all the time when I was a child. At school I was always drawn to the kids who had some link to abroad and I wanted to find out more. I got to study languages at school and university eventually, and it grew from there. Today, my daily life is multilingual. I often get mistaken for other nationalities and I honestly no longer regard nationality as important. It seems almost odd for me to talk about being just British now. Learning languages is an endless and ongoing process for me, which I intend to continue for as many years as my body and mind will allow. When I'm really in the learning zone, my focus is narrow and I try to forget about my other languages. If I didn't, I'd go mad. I simply start a new language and don't think about the others, unless I see obvious links to help the learning process and to understand grammar.

C Anthony Fields

I used to spend long summers in Greece and Japan as a child, trying to play with the other kids, but none of them spoke any English. It struck me how nice it would be to be able to talk to anybody in the world, regardless of what language they spoke. Pronunciation is the most important thing for me. So I start off really basic, focusing on that. Once I feel more confident, I move on to music from the language to tune in further. The dead time when you're on a bus or doing any mundane task is ideal for squeezing in crucial subconscious language learning, which will pay off in the long run. Learning new languages never stops: there is always more to learn. But my student days are almost over and the prospect of searching for a career is looming closer – so I am thinking about taking a couple of languages to a much higher level. Speaking other languages at native level is an entirely different task to just being a polyglot.

D Liam Clarke

I did poorly in languages in school. I barely passed German and, until I was 21, I only spoke English. I moved to Spain after graduating; after six months, I still hadn't learned any Spanish. I kept telling myself that I didn't have the language gene. Eventually, I decided to put my excuses aside and dive in. It took a while, but as soon as I had a basic conversation, I got hooked. That was ten years ago, and since then I've travelled the world, learning many languages. I don't think visiting the country where the language is spoken is really that necessary nowadays, because of the internet. But if you do travel, it opens a lot of interesting doors. I recently had a birthday lunch with four generations of Italians, for example. No way would that have happened if I'd only spoken English. The initial stage is the hardest, but the only real way to get through this is to grin and bear it. I've learned to ignore the fact that I'm making mistakes. That confidence allows me to strive for the next level.

WRITING (1 hour 30 minutes)

Part 1

You **must** answer this question. Write your answer in **220–260** words in an appropriate style.

1 Your class has listened to a radio discussion about different ways of looking after young children. You have made the notes below:

Ways of looking after young children:
- at home with parents or other family members
- in nurseries or pre-schools
- with a professional nanny

Some opinions expressed in the discussion:

"Children develop best when they spend a lot of time with their family."

"It's important for children to learn to get along with other children."

"Nannies are trained to deal with all sorts of situations."

Write an essay for your tutor discussing **two** of the ways of looking after young children in your notes. You should **explain which way is more beneficial** and **provide reasons** to support your opinion.

You may, if you wish, make use of the opinions expressed in the discussion, but you should use your own words as far as possible.

Part 2

Write an answer to **one** of the questions **2–4** in this part. Write your answer in **220–260** words in an appropriate style.

---

2   An international lifestyle magazine has published an article which argues that pop music contributes nothing to people's lives. You have read the article and think that its ideas are too negative. Write a letter to the magazine editor in which you explain your reasons for disagreeing with the article, giving your opinion on the value of pop music in people's lives today.

Write your **letter**. You do not need to include postal addresses.

3   The international company where you work has recently developed a new product. Your manager has asked you to write a report about this for Head Office. You should briefly describe the product, evaluate how successful it has been so far in your region and suggest ways in which more customers could be attracted to purchase the new product.

Write your **report**.

4   A website has asked users to write reviews of unusual leisure activities they have tried. Your review should describe what the activity was, commenting on how far it met your expectations. You should also explain what kind of person might find this activity particularly enjoyable.

Write your **review**.

LISTENING (approximately 40 minutes)

Part 1

You will hear three different extracts.

For questions **1–6**, choose the answer (**A**, **B** or **C**) which fits best according to what you hear. There are two questions for each extract.

Extract One

You hear part of a radio interview with a product designer called Charles Loughlan.

1   How does Charles feel about designers who put their names on products?

    A He understands their basic needs.

    B He is dismissive of their motives.

    C He admires their business skills.

2   What does Charles suggest about a good product?

    A Its appearance should reflect its function.

    B It should encourage a desire to possess it.

    C Its ecological impact should be considered.

Extract Two

You hear two friends discussing a TV interview with an actress called Celia Dent.

3   They agree that the interviewer made the mistake of

    A dominating the discussion.

    B asking predictable questions.

    C failing to listen fully to answers.

4   The man says that certain film stars can be difficult to interview because

    A they generally show a lack of spontaneity.

    B they're unwilling to reveal their true personality.

    C they're too anxious to promote their latest work.

Extract Three

You hear two freelance journalists talking about their work.

5   When talking about how he tackles a creative writing task, the man

   A   points out how easily he can assume the right frame of mind.

   B   tries to justify his antisocial behaviour when working.

   C   admits that frequent breaks can be beneficial.

6   What does the woman say about her earlier writing?

   A   She feels she no longer fully relates to it.

   B   She tends to draw on similar themes in her current work.

   C   She highlights the improvements she's noticed in her work.

Part 2

You will hear a woman called Janine Rogers giving a talk about her work. For questions **7–14**, complete the sentences with a word or short phrase.

Working with Chocolate

Janine trained as a **(7)** .... before working for her current employer.

Janine found her background particularly helpful when working on a project to put

(8) .... into chocolate.

Janine uses the word **(9)** .... to describe chocolate as a

substance to work with.

Janine mentions the method of **(10)** .... the cocoa beans as

a variable affecting the taste of her chocolate.

Janine says that ideas for new types of chocolate generally come from her company's

(11) .... department.

Janine says the staff responsible for **(12)** .... play a

surprisingly important role in developing a new chocolate product.

Janine gives the example of **(13)** .... as a group that need to

be considered when designing the label for a product.

Janine thinks that **(14)** .... is the most essential quality needed for her job.

Part 3

You will hear part of an interview with two sports psychologists called Sheila Forbes and Peter Maxton. For questions **15–20**, choose the answer (**A**, **B**, **C** or **D**) which fits best according to what you hear.

15   Sheila explains that her role involves
    A   preventing players from becoming over-confident.
    B   responding to whatever players feel they need to improve.
    C   enabling players to train aggressively.
    D   persuading players that her techniques can really benefit them.

16   Sheila says one strategy she uses to achieve her goals is to
    A   encourage players to replicate good features of others' performance.
    B   ask players to share with her the way they control their anxieties.
    C   get players to examine their effectiveness as team members.
    D   trace the causes of negative thinking in players.

17   Sheila and Peter both think that it's important for sports psychologists
    A   to have wide experience in a range of different sports.
    B   not to raise false hopes about what they can achieve.
    C   not to become too immersed in the environment of sport.
    D   to adapt the decisions they make to suit individual situations.

18   What was Peter's reaction to his deteriorating sporting performance as a student?
    A   He felt disappointed at the lack of relevant help available.
    B   He redoubled his efforts to succeed despite failing health.
    C   He became desperate to uncover the source of his problem.
    D   He switched to what he felt were easier sports to succeed in.

19   What does Peter dislike about his job?
    A   needing always to be creative in his choice of techniques
    B   having constantly to work in different environments
    C   being criticised for ineffective working methods
    D   feeling he has to justify his achievements to others

20   When talking about their profession, Shelia and Peter agree that
    A   it's slowly establishing its place in player development.
    B   it isn't attracting the right kind of people.
    C   its profile needs to be raised among the general public.
    D   it has a poorly-developed career structure.

Part 4

You will hear five short extracts in which students are talking about their universities.

TASK ONE

For questions **21–25**, choose from the list (**A–H**) the reason each speaker gives for choosing their university.

TASK TWO

For questions **26–30**, choose from the list (**A–H**) what each speaker found hardest at the start of their first year at university.

While you listen, you must complete both tasks.

A	a personal recommendation
B	a modern facility
C	family pressure
D	its convenient location
E	the support network provided
F	its international reputation
G	its distinctive architecture
H	the range of courses on offer

Speaker 1	21
Speaker 2	22
Speaker 3	23
Speaker 4	24
Speaker 5	25

A	keeping up with the workload
B	getting on with fellow students
C	understanding the academic content
D	finding something to do at weekends
E	locating lecture venues
F	dealing with domestic tasks
G	getting used to a new schedule
H	finding a suitable place to study

Speaker 1	26
Speaker 2	27
Speaker 3	28
Speaker 4	29
Speaker 5	30

SPEAKING (15 minutes)

There are two examiners. One (the interlocutor) conducts the test, providing you with the necessary materials and explaining what you have to do. The other examiner (the assessor) is introduced to you, but then takes no further part in the interaction.

Part 1 (2 minutes)

The interlocutor first asks you and your partner for some information about yourselves, then widens the scope of the questions by asking about e.g. your leisure activities, studies, travel and daily life. You are expected to respond to the interlocutor's questions and listen to what your partner has to say.

Part 2 (a one-minute 'long turn' for each candidate, plus a 30-second response from the second candidate)

You are each given the opportunity to talk for about a minute, and to comment briefly after your partner has spoken.

The interlocutor gives you a set of three pictures and asks you to talk about two of them for about one minute. It is important to listen carefully to the interlocutor's instructions. The interlocutor then asks your partner a question about your pictures and your partner responds briefly.

You are then given another set of pictures to look at. Your partner talks about these pictures for about one minute. This time the interlocutor asks you a question about your partner's pictures and you respond briefly.

Part 3 (4 minutes)

In this part of the test, you and your partner are asked to talk together. The interlocutor places a question and some text prompts on the table between you. This stimulus provides the basis for a discussion, after which you will need to make a decision on the topic in question. The interlocutor explains what you have to do.

Part 4 (5 minutes)

The interlocutor asks some further questions, which leads to a more general discussion of the topic you have discussed in Part 3. You may comment on your partner's answers if you wish.

Frames for the Speaking Test

Test 5

Note: In the examination, there will be both an assessor and an interlocutor in the exam. The visual material for **Test 5** appears on pages C1 and C2 (Part 2) and C3 (Part 3).

Part 1   2 minutes (3 minutes for groups of three)

Interlocutor: Good morning/afternoon/evening. My name is ………… and this is my colleague, …………．

And your names are?

Can I have your mark sheets, please?

Thank you.

First of all we'd like to know something about you.

Select one or two questions and ask candidates in turn, as appropriate.

- Where are you from?
- What do you do here/there?
- How long have you been studying English?
- What do you enjoy most about learning English?

Select one or more questions for each candidate, as appropriate.

- What do you think is the best thing about life in your country? ….. (Why?)
- How important is it for you to keep fit? ….. (Why?)
- Do you enjoy socialising with a large group of people? ….. (Why? / Why not?)
- What would you do if you had more free time on weekdays?
- How do you prefer to travel in your home town?
- What preparations do you usually make before you go on a holiday or trip?
- Would you call yourself an optimistic person? ….. (Why? / Why not?)
- Would you mind doing a job which involved some evening work? ….. (Why? / Why not?)

Part 2   4 minutes (6 minutes for groups of three)

Isolated places

Painting

Interlocutor:	In this part of the test, I'm going to give each of you three pictures. I'd like you to talk about **two** of them on your own for about a minute, and also to answer a question briefly about your partner's pictures.
	(Candidate A), it's your turn first. Here are your pictures. They show **people in isolated places.**
	Indicate the pictures on page C1 to the candidates.
	I'd like you to compare **two** of the pictures, and say **why the people might have chosen to be in these isolated places, and what problems they might face.**
	All right?
Candidate A:	[*1 minute*]
Interlocutor:	Thank you.
	(Candidate B), **who might enjoy being in this isolated situation the most?** ...... **(Why?)**
Candidate B:	[*Approximately 30 seconds*]
Interlocutor:	Thank you.
	Now, *(Candidate B),* here are your pictures. They show **people painting for different reasons.**
	Indicate the pictures on page C2 to the candidates.
	I'd like you to compare **two** of the pictures, and say **what skills the people might need to do this painting, and how enjoyable the activity might be.**
	All right?
Candidate B:	[*1 minute*]
Interlocutor:	Thank you.
	(Candidate A), **who do you think will finish their painting first?** ...... **(Why?)**
Candidate A:	[*Approximately 30 seconds*]
Interlocutor:	Thank you.

Part 3   4 minutes (6 minutes for groups of three)

Part 4   5 minutes (8 minutes for groups of three)
Being supportive

Part 3

Interlocutor:	Now, I'd like you to talk about something together for about two minutes *(3 minutes for groups of three)*.
	Here are some areas of life where people might need help and support from others and a question for you to discuss. First you have some time to look at the task.
	Indicate the text prompts on C3 to the candidates. Allow 15 seconds.
	Now, talk to each other about **what sort of help and support people might need from others in these different areas of life, and why.**
Candidates:	[*2 minutes (3 minutes for groups of three)*]
Interlocutor:	Thank you. Now you have about a minute *(2 minutes for groups of three)* to decide **in which area people need least support.**
Candidates:	[*1 minute (2 minutes for groups of three)*]
Interlocutor:	Thank you.

Part 4

Interlocutor: *Use the following questions, in order, as appropriate:*

- What sort of qualities do you think people need in order to be able to give good help and advice to others? ...... (Why? / Why not?)
- Why do you think some people don't look for support from others? ...... (Why? / Why not?)
- Some people say it is easier to help strangers rather than people you know. What's your opinion? ...... (Why? / Why not?)
- Who do you think should provide care for elderly people, the government or their families? ...... (Why? / Why not?)
- Is it more important to encourage people to find their own solutions to problems rather than give them the answers? ...... (Why? / Why not?)
- Who do you usually go to for advice, your friends or your family? ...... (Why? / Why not?)

Select any of the following prompts, as appropriate:

- What do you think?
- Do you agree?
- How about you?

Thank you. That is the end of the test.

Test 6

Note: In the examination, there will be both an assessor and an interlocutor in the exam. The visual material for **Test 6** appears on pages C4 and C5 (Part 2) and C6 (Part 3).

Part 1   2 minutes (3 minutes for groups of three)

Interlocutor: Good morning/afternoon/evening. My name is .... and this is my colleague, ...

And your names are?

Can I have your mark sheets, please?

Thank you.

First of all we'd like to know something about you.

Select one or two questions and ask candidates in turn, as appropriate.

- Where are you from?
- What do you do here/there?
- How long have you been studying English?
- What do you enjoy most about learning English?

Select one or more questions for each candidate, as appropriate.

- What do you think is the best thing about life in your country? ..... (Why?)
- How important is it for you to keep fit? ..... (Why?)
- Do you enjoy socialising with a large group of people? ..... (Why? / Why not?)
- What would you do if you had more free time on weekdays?
- How do you prefer to travel in your home town?
- What preparations do you usually make before you go on a holiday or trip?
- Would you call yourself an optimistic person? ..... (Why? / Why not?)
- Would you mind doing a job which involved some evening work? ..... (Why? / Why not?)

Part 2 4 minutes (6 minutes for groups of three)

Celebrating

Checking information

Interlocutor:	In this part of the test, I'm going to give each of you three pictures. I'd like you to talk about **two** of them on your own for about a minute, and also to answer a question briefly about your partner's pictures.
	(Candidate A), it's your turn first. Here are your pictures. They show **people celebrating different things.**
	Indicate the pictures on page C4 to the candidates.
	I'd like you to compare **two** of the pictures, and say **what these people might be celebrating, and how long they might have prepared for these celebrations.**
	All right?
Candidate A:	[*1 minute*]
Interlocutor:	Thank you.
	(Candidate B), **which celebration do you think would be the most memorable?** …… (**Why?**)
Candidate B:	[*Approximately 30 seconds*]
Interlocutor:	Thank you.
	Now, *(Candidate B)*, here are your pictures. They show **people checking information in different situations.**
	Indicate the pictures on page C5 to the candidates.
	I'd like you to compare **two** of the pictures, and say **why they might be checking this information, and how useful the information might be.**
	All right?
Candidate B:	[*1 minute*]
Interlocutor:	Thank you.
	(Candidate A), **who do you think needs to check the information most carefully?** …… (**Why?**)
Candidate A:	[*Approximately 30 seconds*]
Interlocutor:	Thank you.

Part 3   4 minutes (6 minutes for groups of three)

Part 4   5 minutes (8 minutes for groups of three)

Following rules

Part 3

Interlocutor:	Now, I'd like you to talk about something together for about two minutes *(3 minutes for groups of three)*.
	Here are some areas of life where people are expected to follow rules and a question for you to discuss. First you have some time to look at the task.
	Indicate the text prompts on C6 to the candidates. Allow 15 seconds.
	Now, talk to each other about how **important it is to follow the rules in these different areas of life.**
Candidates:	[*2 minutes (3 minutes for groups of three)*]
Interlocutor:	Thank you. Now you have about a minute *(2 minutes for groups of three)* to decide **which area of life needs rules the most.**
Candidates:	[*1 minute (2 minutes for groups of three)*]
Interlocutor:	Thank you.

Part 4

Interlocutor: *Use the following questions, in order, as appropriate:*

> *Select any of the following prompts, as appropriate:*
> - What do you think?
> - Do you agree?
> - How about you?

- Some people say there are too many rules in our lives these days. Do you agree? ...... (Why? / Why not?)
- How important do you think it is to learn the difference between right and wrong at an early age? ...... (Why? / Why not?)
- Do you think it's always important to obey rules? ...... (Why? / Why not?)
- Do you think that having security cameras in towns and cities is a good way of making sure people follow the rules? ...... (Why? / Why not?)
- Some people like to have rules and routines in their lives. Why do you think this is?
- If there was one rule you could change, what would it be and why?

Thank you. That is the end of the test.

Test 7

Note: In the examination, there will be both an assessor and an interlocutor in the exam. The visual material for **Test 7** appears on pages C7 and C8 (Part 2) and C9 (Part 3).

Part 1   2 minutes (3 minutes for groups of three)

Interlocutor: Good morning/afternoon/evening. My name is ………… and this is my colleague, ………… .

And your names are?

Can I have your mark sheets, please?

Thank you.

First of all we'd like to know something about you.

Select one or two questions and ask candidates in turn, as appropriate.

- Where are you from?
- What do you do here/there?
- How long have you been studying English?
- What do you enjoy most about learning English?

Select one or more questions for each candidate, as appropriate.

- If you could live anywhere in the world, where would it be? (Why?)
- Do you enjoy organising parties? (Why? / Why not?)
- What do you like to do in your spare time? (Why?)
- How important do you think it is to follow the news from around the world? (Why? / Why not?)
- Is there an event in your home town which you particularly enjoy? (Why?)
- Would you say that you are a tidy person? (Why? / Why not?)
- Do you think you study best when you're in a group? (Why?)
- What are your plans for the next few months?

Part 2   4 minutes (6 minutes for groups of three)

Help and encouragement

Collecting things

Interlocutor:	In this part of the test, I'm going to give each of you three pictures. I'd like you to talk about **two** of them on your own for about a minute, and also to answer a question briefly about your partner's pictures.
	(Candidate A), it's your turn first. Here are your pictures. They show **people giving help and encouragement in different situations.**
	Indicate the pictures on page C7 to the candidates.
	I'd like you to compare **two** of the pictures, and say **what sort of help and encouragement the people are giving in these situations, and how useful this might be.**
	All right?
Candidate A:	[*1 minute*]
Interlocutor:	Thank you.
	(Candidate B), **who do you think will benefit most from the help and encouragement?** ...... **(Why?)**
Candidate B:	[*Approximately 30 seconds*]
Interlocutor:	Thank you.
	Now, *(Candidate B)*, here are your pictures. They show **people collecting different things.**
	Indicate the pictures on page C8 to the candidates.
	I'd like you to compare two of the pictures, and say **why you think the people are collecting these things, and what satisfaction they might get from doing this.**
	All right?
Candidate B:	[*1 minute*]
Interlocutor:	Thank you.
	(Candidate A), **who do you think needs to be the most careful when collecting?** ...... **(Why?)**
Candidate A:	[*Approximately 30 seconds*]
Interlocutor:	Thank you.

Part 3 4 minutes (6 minutes for groups of three)

Part 4 5 minutes (8 minutes for groups of three)

Making decisions

Part 3

Interlocutor:	Now, I'd like you to talk about something together for about two minutes *(3 minutes for groups of three)*.
	Here are some things that people need to make decisions about and a question for you to discuss. First you have some time to look at the task.
	Indicate the text prompts on C9 to the candidates. Allow 15 seconds.
	Now, talk to each other about **how important it is to get advice when making decisions about these things and why.**
Candidates:	[*2 minutes (3 minutes for groups of three)*]
Interlocutor:	Thank you. Now you have about a minute *(2 minutes for groups of three)* to decide **which of these things it is most important to think about carefully.**
Candidates:	[*1 minute (2 minutes for groups of three)*]
Interlocutor:	Thank you.

Part 4

Interlocutor: *Use the following questions, in order, as appropriate:*

- Some people say that we learn a lot from the mistakes we make. What do you think? ...... (Why? / Why not?)
- Do you think it is possible to teach people to make the right decisions about things? ...... (Why? / Why not?)
- Do you think that once you've made a decision you shouldn't change your mind? ...... (Why? / Why not?)
- Many parents find it difficult to let their children become independent. What's your opinion? ...... (Why? / Why not?)
- Some people say it's getting harder and harder to find time to do everything they want. What do you think? ...... (Why? / Why not?)
- Some people think it's important to have control over everything in their lives. What's your opinion?

> *Select any of the following prompts, as appropriate:*
> - What do you think?
> - Do you agree?
> - How about you?

Thank you. That is the end of the test.

Test 8

Note: In the examination, there will be both an assessor and an interlocutor in the exam. The visual material for **Test 8** appears on pages C10 and C11 (Part 2) and C12 (Part 3).

Part 1   2 minutes (3 minutes for groups of three)

Interlocutor:	Good morning/afternoon/evening. My name is ………… and this is my colleague, …………. .

And your names are?

Can I have your mark sheets, please?

Thank you.

First of all we'd like to know something about you.

Select one or two questions and ask candidates in turn, as appropriate.

- Where are you from?
- What do you do here/there?
- How long have you been studying English?
- What do you enjoy most about learning English?

Select one or more questions for each candidate, as appropriate.

- If you could live anywhere in the world, where would it be? (Why?)
- Do you enjoy organising parties? (Why? / Why not?)
- What do you like to do in your spare time? (Why?)
- How important do you think it is to follow the news from around the world? (Why? / Why not?)
- Is there an event in your home town which you particularly enjoy? (Why?)
- Would you say that you are a tidy person? (Why? / Why not?)
- Do you think you study best when you're in a group? (Why?)
- What are your plans for the next few months?

Part 2   4 minutes (6 minutes for groups of three)

Annoying situations

Looking carefully

Interlocutor:	In this part of the test, I'm going to give each of you three pictures. I'd like you to talk about **two** of them on your own for about a minute, and also to answer a question briefly about your partner's pictures.
	(Candidate A), it's your turn first. Here are your pictures. They show **people in annoying situations.**
	Indicate the pictures on page C10 to the candidates.
	I'd like you to compare **two** of the pictures, and say **what can be annoying in these different situations, and what might happen next.**
	All right?
Candidate A:	[*1 minute*]
Interlocutor:	Thank you.
	(Candidate B), **who do you think will be most affected by the situation?** ...... **(Why?)**
Candidate B:	[*Approximately 30 seconds*]
Interlocutor:	Thank you.
	Now, *(Candidate B)*, here are your pictures. They show **people looking at different things.**
	Indicate the pictures on page C11 to the candidates.
	I'd like you to compare **two** of the pictures, and say **why the people might be looking at these things, and how important it is for them to look at these things carefully.**
	All right?
Candidate B:	[*1 minute*]
Interlocutor:	Thank you.
	(Candidate A), **who do you think needs to concentrate the most?** ...... **(Why?)**
Candidate A:	[*Approximately 30 seconds*]
Interlocutor:	Thank you.

Part 3   4 minutes (6 minutes for groups of three)

Part 4   5 minutes (8 minutes for groups of three)

Working together in a team

Part 3

Interlocutor:	Now, I'd like you to talk about something together for about two minutes *(3 minutes for groups of three)*.
	Here are some things that people think are important when working together in a team and a question for you to discuss. First you have some time to look at the task.
	Indicate the text prompts on C12 to the candidates. Allow 15 seconds.
	Now, talk to each other about **how these things can affect the experience of working together in a team.**
Candidates:	[*2 minutes (3 minutes for groups of three)*]
Interlocutor:	Thank you. Now you have about a minute *(2 minutes for groups of three)* to decide **which of these things would have the greatest positive effect on working in a team.**
Candidates:	[*1 minute (2 minutes for groups of three)*]
Interlocutor:	Thank you.

Part 4

Interlocutor: *Use the following questions, in order, as appropriate:*

Select any of the following prompts, as appropriate:
- What do you think?
- Do you agree?
- How about you?

- Do you think that getting and giving feedback on each other's work is always a good thing? ...... (Why? / Why not?)
- Some people say that working in a team can produce better results than working individually? Do you agree? ...... (Why? / Why not?)
- Do you think it benefits companies if they arrange social activities for their staff? ...... (Why? / Why not?)
- Some people feel that work always needs to be challenging. What do you think? ...... (Why? / Why not?)
- In your opinion, do people's attitudes to work change as they become more successful? ...... (Why? / Why not?)
- Do you think people will spend a longer or shorter time at work in the future? ...... (Why?)

Thank you. That is the end of the test.

Marks and results

Reading and Use of English

Candidates record their answers on a separate answer sheet. One mark is given for each correct answer in Parts 1, 2 and 3 and up to two marks are given for each correct answer in Part 4. For Parts 5, 6 and 7 two marks are given for each correct answer and in Part 8 one mark is given for each correct answer. Candidates will receive separate scores for Reading and for Use of English. The total marks candidates achieve for each section are converted into a score on the Cambridge English Scale. These are equally weighted when calculating the overall score on the scale (an average of the individual scores for the four skills and Use of English).

Writing

Examiners look at four aspects of a candidate's writing: Content, Communicative Achievement, Organisation and Language. The total mark is converted into a score on the Cambridge English Scale for the paper.

- **Content** focuses on how well the candidate has fulfilled the task; in other words if they have done what they were asked to do.
- **Communicative Achievement** focuses on how appropriate the writing is for the situation and whether the candidate has used the appropriate register.
- **Organisation** focuses on the way the piece of writing was put together; in other words if it is logical and ordered, and the punctuation is correct.
- **Language** focuses on the candidate's vocabulary and grammar. This includes the range of language as well as how accurate it is.

For each of the subscales, the examiner gives a maximum of 5 marks. Examiners use the following assessment scale:

C1	Content	Communicative Achievement	Organisation	Language
5	All content is relevant to the task. Target reader is fully informed.	Uses the conventions of the communicative task with sufficient flexibility to communicate complex ideas in an effective way, holding the target reader's attention with ease, fulfilling all communicative purposes.	Text is a well organised, coherent whole, using a variety of cohesive devices and organisational patterns with flexibility.	Uses a range of vocabulary, including less common lexis, effectively and precisely. Uses a wide range of simple and complex grammatical forms with full control, flexibility and sophistication. Errors, if present, are related to less common words and structures, or are slips.

4	*Performance shares features of Bands 3 and 5.*			
3	Minor irrelevances and/or omissions may be present. Target reader is, on the whole, informed.	Uses the conventions of the communicative task effectively to hold the target reader's attention and communicate straightforward and complex ideas, as appropriate.	Text is well organised and coherent, using a variety of cohesive devices and organisational patterns to generally good effect.	Uses a range of vocabulary, including less common lexis, appropriately. Uses a range of simple and complex grammatical forms with control and flexibility. Occasional errors may be present but do not impede communication.
2	*Performance shares features of Bands 1 and 3.*			
1	Irrelevances and misinterpretation of task may be present. Target reader is minimally informed.	Uses the conventions of the communicative task to hold the target reader's attention and communicate straightforward ideas.	Text is generally well organised and coherent, using a variety of linking words and cohesive devices.	Uses a range of everyday vocabulary appropriately, with occasional inappropriate use of less common lexis. Uses a range of simple and some complex grammatical forms with a good degree of control. Errors do not impede communication.
0	Content is totally irrelevant. Target reader is not informed.	Performance below Band 1.		

Length of responses

Candidates need to make sure that they write the correct number of words. Responses which are too short may not have an adequate range of language and may not provide all the information that is required. Responses which are too long may contain irrelevant content and have a negative effect on the reader.

Varieties of English

Candidates are expected to use a particular variety of English with some degree of consistency in areas such as spelling, and not for example switch from using a British spelling of a word to an American spelling of the same word.

Sample A (Test 5, Question 1 – Essay)

Young people living in cities

Nowadays many young people prefer to live in the big cities. There are many factors that have influence on their decision, but the most common are work and education.

It is the job that really matters to all of us and especially to the young generation. They all want a high salary, which will provide them a good and stable life. But as we know the wider range of jobs can be found in the big cities and that is why young people choose to live there.

The other reason, which is really important for students, is the education. Most of the good universities are located in the cities and the young have no choice, because the majority realise that if you want to succeed in the life, you need to have an excellent education.

Also the educational system is better in towns than in villages. A bigger variety of programmes is available and you can have a chance to get an internship, which will be really helpful in the future when you are trying to find a good job.

Of course, there are more reasons like night life, that will always attract the young people to choose the big city than the small one. However, the work and the education will be the most important, because they have a vital importance in the life of all of us.

Scales	Mark	Commentary
Content	3	Two factors – work and education – are discussed but no choice is made as to which is more important (with supporting reasons); the target reader is on the whole informed.
Communicative Achievement	4	Essay conventions are used with sufficient flexibility to communicate straightforward and complex ideas in an effective way. The register is appropriate.
Organisation	4	Well organised with clear opening and closing sections. Ideas are presented logically, each paragraph developing a new point. Cohesive devices and organisational patterns, such as referencing, are used naturally and effectively to link ideas within and across paragraphs creating a coherent text. Accurate punctuation.
Language	3	There is a range of vocabulary, including less common lexis, used appropriately (*'influence on their decision'*, *'provide … a stable life'*, *'a chance to get an internship'*, *'a vital importance'*) and a range of simple and complex grammatical forms used with control (*'if you want to succeed …, you need to have …'*, *'which will be useful … when you are trying to find …'*). The occasional errors do not impede communication.

Sample B (Test 5, Question 4 – Proposal)

> PROPOSAL OF SPANISH STUDENTS INVITATION
>
> Introduction
>
> The aim of this proposal is to suggest some ways of raising up the students visits so as to make profit from it in the future.
>
> Two weeks visit
>
> Many international colleges around the world organise visits, in which all nationalities can be participating. It would be interesting to send an invitation to some students from my born country, Spain. Although these kind of events are expensive, our college could afford it if the visit lastes about two weeks, not more.
>
> A wide range of activities could be hold, such as baseball match, an intensive course with our teachers or a London tour, which foreing people usually love.
>
> Benefits
>
> Not only would the students learnt the language, but also could the college offer them a hole year pack, in which they will find all kind of activities to meet new people. Moreover, the new students will know more about the country culture.
>
> Regarding the current students, they could take part in all the activities that the news ones will do. So it will be several positive points.
>
> Recommendations
>
> I think that if the college takes into consideration these suggestions, a marked improvent will be in the public image of it.

Scales	Mark	Commentary
Content	5	All content is relevant to the task and the content elements (length of visit, description of activities and explanation of potential benefits) are developed appropriately so the target reader is fully informed.
Communicative Achievement	2	Suitable proposal format is used to communicate straightforward and some complex ideas to the target reader. Register and tone are consistent and appropriate.
Organisation	3	The response is well organised and coherent, making good use of headings. A variety of cohesive devices and organisational patterns connect the text generally very well.
Language	2	There is a range of vocabulary including attempts, sometimes successful, to use less common lexis (*'raising up the visits'*, *'make profit from it'*, *'a marked improvement … in the public image …'*). There is a range of simple and some complex grammatical forms used with a good degree of control and errors do not impede communication.

Sample C (Test 6, Question 2 – Report)

> ### Report on college study resources
>
> Introduction
>
> The aim of this report is to evaluate a range of study resources available for students majoring in 'English and Marketing' programme and recommend possible improvements.
>
> English Course
>
> In terms of language learning, I highly appreciate the set of text books that the students were provided with due to a wide variety of discussion topics as well as high-quality supplementary materials for self-study such as interactive CD-roms and extensive word lists. All this has proved to be vital resources for the ones who strive to acquire an excellent command of the English language.
>
> Marketing Course
>
> As far as the subjects in the marketing field are concerned, I suppose the selected study materials are a bit too theoretical. Although the students stand at a chance to master Business English fully during their extensive reading, the materials miss out on more practical issues, for instance, lacking in such as valuable resource as case-studies. As a result, the students had a relatively limited number of opportunities to see how the suggested marketing solutions could be implemented into practice.
>
> Recommendations
>
> Given the advanced software solutions, I would suggest introducing more computer-based self-study materials with more control on the tutor's part if possible both in language learning and marketing courses. To improve the latter, I would strongly recommend providing students with more sample cases, which will be entirely beneficial for developing their project work.

Scales	Mark	Commentary
Content	5	The writer develops both content areas describing what study resources are offered to students and suggesting improvements for next year. All the content is relevant and the target reader is fully informed.
Communicative Achievement	4	The conventions of report writing are used flexibly to describe the current situation in some detail and make credible suggestions. The register is consistently appropriate and a positive, constructive tone is created which holds the reader's attention while communicating complex ideas.
Organisation	4	The text is a well-organised, coherent whole with effective use of headed sections. A variety of cohesive devices and organisational patterns is used to good effect.
Language	4	The writer includes a range of topic-specific vocabulary (*'vital resources'*, *'strive to acquire'*, *'chance to master'*, *'extensive reading'*, *'relatively limited number of opportunities'*, *'could be implemented'*), which is generally used effectively and precisely. There is a range of complex grammatical forms used with control and where there are errors, some are slips. None of them impedes communication.

Sample D (Test 6, Question 3 – Review)

When our coach told us that we were going to a swimming camp in Canarian Islands during the recent summer holidays, none of us was looking forward to it nor very excited about the idea, as that would mean metres and metres of swimming in lakes in the middle of nowhere and running under extreme temperatures. But the experience turned out to be a great opportunity not only to improve our swimming skills, but also to have a good time with our team mates, coaches and members of the club staff and as a bonus, to have a go at some alternative sports.

Consisting of around ten residence blocks for guests and a huge range of sport facilities, including an olimpic swimming pool, the premises were just what our team was looking for. At the end of the day, a huge amount of money had been invested in the experience so that it was well worth going.

We went for a routine run every morning before the sunrise. I have to admit that running 10km every day without even having had breakfast is not the nicest thing to do, but we were there to work out hard and the instructors were so enthusiastic and supportive that they made it easier for us to get motivated.

I would recommend this type of break to everyone keen on sports, especially thriatlon, swimming and surfing, but taking into consideration that being fit and in physically good condition is a priority to be able to make the most of the activities.

Scales	Mark	Commentary
Content	5	All content is relevant to the task. The three areas specified in the rubric are included and developed appropriately, so the target reader is fully informed.
Communicative Achievement	4	The conventions of review writing are used to convey complex ideas effectively and flexibly. The tone and register are consistently appropriate for a travel magazine article and language of description, evaluation and opinion is used to hold the target reader's attention.
Organisation	3	The text is well organised and coherent. It starts with an introduction to the holiday, moving on to evaluate the positive and negative aspects and concluding with a recommendation. Clearly paragraphed with attention paid to punctuation and a variety of cohesive devices and organisational patterns used to generally good effect.
Language	4	A range of vocabulary is used, generally effectively and precisely (*'in the middle of nowhere'*, *'extreme temperatures'*, *'alternative sports'*, *'well worth going'*, *'a huge amount of money had been invested in the experience'*). Complex grammatical forms are used with control and flexibility (*'were just what our team was looking for'*, *'running every day without even having had breakfast ...'*). The occasional errors do not impede communication.

Sample E (Test 7, Question 2 – Letter)

Dear Jack,

In my experience in the Netherlands technology is hugely important in education. Here, in my school, everybody uses laptops and all classrooms are equipped with beamers and audio boxes. It opens up a lot of different methods of learning! We can watch documentaries in classes like Economics, and films in classes like French or history.

We use our laptops in combination with servers the school has set up and on those servers is a lot of information. Study planners for every subject, homework assignments and test results, for example. It's very handy, always being able to access stuff like that, all you need is a computer and an internet connection! The latter can give some problems though, as technical errors are bound to happen every once in a while. Just last Friday we got send home because the internet wasn't working, and thus nobody could access anything! That's the only major disadvantage to all the technology we have adopted into our classrooms.

Our dependency on it has become a bit too big in my opinion. We should be able to continue classes even without our internet connection. While learning with digital material is great, we needn't forget our paper books. Personally I prefer reading from a book to reading off a computer screen any day of the week.

I hope I have given you some kind of answer in this email, but in case I haven't, feel free to let me know. I'll gladly elaborate.

Untill next time,

Scales	Mark	Commentary
Content	5	All content is relevant to the task. All the rubric elements are addressed and developed so the target reader is fully informed.
Communicative Achievement	5	The conventions of letter writing are used flexibly to explain and justify the writer's views and the engaging tone throughout holds the reader's attention. Complex ideas are communicated clearly.
Organisation	4	The text is a well-organised, coherent whole using a variety of cohesive devices. Organisational patterns are used to generally good effect. The paragraphing works well as each one has a different focus and punctuation is used effectively.
Language	4	Uses a range of task-appropriate vocabulary effectively and accurately (*'opens up', 'in combination with servers', 'very handy', 'technical errors are bound to happen', 'our dependency on it'*). There is a range of simple and complex grammatical forms used with flexibility and control. The occasional errors do not impede communication.

Sample F (Test 7, Question 4 – Review)

'Der Schuh Des Manitu'

Films are typically produced in America or in India. Although German cinemas show American Hollywood films, German productions can be interesting and funny too. One quiet famous one is the "Der Schuh des Manito", which is a comedy film playing in a fictional wild western world. The German actors are very popular in German and even Hollywood movies, that's why this movie is so famous.

Looking at the production and studio work of the movie, it is quite authentic and can be compared to a Hollywood movie. In fact the movie is based on an actual Western movie. The actual movie is a Hollywood production called "Winetu" so the German movie "Der Schuh des Manito" is some kind of parody, without actually offending the real story.

The humor of the movie is a little bit different to most US movies. German humor is special anyways and this movie presents it really well. To some people it may seem stupid or silly, but in general most people will find something interesting and funny about it.

Looking at the making of the movie and the stunts, you can see that it is a proffessional work, which can't always be stated for German films. I believe the movie has great potential for an international audience, since it is a worthful production with a lot of humor. Since it is a fictional movie or actually based on a US story, the movie would be pretty popular in the US, Europe, Asia, Australia and even Africa. To sum it up 'Der Schuh Des Manito' shows that German movies can be good and worth watching.

Scales	Mark	Commentary
Content	5	All content is relevant to the task. The writer addresses and develops all the content areas so the target reader is fully informed.
Communicative Achievement	3	The conventions of the communicative task are used effectively and the register is consistent and appropriate for a website review. Both simple and complex ideas are conveyed.
Organisation	3	It is well organised and coherent, making good use of paragraphs. A variety of cohesive devices which connect the text generally very well, is used.
Language	3	There is a range of vocabulary including some less common lexis ('*quite authentic*', '*a kind of parody*', '*great potential for an international audience*') and control is shown in the use of simple and complex grammatical structures. The occasional errors are non-impeding.

Sample G (Test 8, Question 1 – Essay)

Nowadays we are surrounded by a lots of different peaces of information on the Internet, in books or magazines and so on, about how to bring up children. But do you know which the most beneficial way for your kids is?

To begin with, some parents would prefer to have their children near them and look after them on their own or with the help of others but still family members. In such situations, the kids would definitely be provided with the love they need in order to grow up in a accommodative atmosphere and develop their personality accurately.

On the other hand, there are many parents that do not have enough time and choose to send their kids in nurseries or pre-schools. Having grown up with other kids, they develop another essential skills such as the ability to communicate with their peers, to make friends and also to cope with various situations which they might come across later in real life. Moreover, being amongs other children, they always have the opportunity to play with them and learn something new while having fun.

In my opinion, the more beneficial way of looking after young kids is in nurseries and pre-schools. It is the communication with people from all walks of life and the experiencing of new and different things, which can't be found in the overprotective atmosphere at home, that will give these little humans a better start for the tough life.

Scales	Mark	Commentary
Content	5	All content is relevant to the task. Two ways of looking after children are discussed and a clear choice made as to which is more beneficial with supporting reasons.
Communicative Achievement	3	Appropriate essay style is used and there is a suitable, consistent register throughout. Ideas are communicated effectively, holding the target reader's attention.
Organisation	4	The text is a well-organised, coherent whole using a variety of cohesive devices and organisational patterns to generally good effect. There is a clear structure with an introduction, discussion of two factors and a developed conclusion. Punctuation is accurate and effective.
Language	3	There is a range of vocabulary used appropriately including some less common lexis ('*cope with various situations*', '*people from all walks of life*', '*overprotective atmosphere*'). There is a range of simple and complex grammatical forms used with control and flexibility. The occasional errors do not impede communication.

Sample H (Test 8, Question 2 – Letter)

Dear Editor,

Your recently published lifestyle magazine contains an article arguing against the contribution of pop music to one's lives. I hereby want to give you some feedback, as you asked for the reader's views.

Music has always been a key part of culture. It offers a vast range of interhuman connections and some even choose their friends soley based on music taste. And as decades and centuries come, wave and pass by, music changes and so does every culture.

We currently face a culture that enjoys what we call 'pop' music; soft and not overly complex melodies paired with simple and repetitive lyrics. But even if the current music taste might seem almost useless, as stated in the article, it still represents our culture.

Today's number one pop song is obviously no match for a well crafted classic piece of art. But music still is a way of expressing emotion. It helps to deal with stress and frustration and builds up happiness and a general mental well-being.

The contribution of music is not hidden behind cryptical yet geniously written stories or the use of real instruments rather than computer generated sounds. The real contribution of music lies both in its nearly endless capabilities of expression and its enormously positive impact on the overall mental well-being.

I hope my feedback is at least of some help and evokes some thoughts on that topic.

Yours sincerely,

Scales	Mark	Commentary
Content	5	All content is relevant to the task. Writer develops both areas – explaining reasons for disagreeing with the article and giving opinions on the value of pop music in people's lives today – so the target reader is fully informed.
Communicative Achievement	5	The conventions of letter writing are used to convey complex ideas and the reader's attention is held with ease. Both register and tone are consistent throughout. The Editor would consider publishing the letter.
Organisation	4	The text is well organised and coherent and the writer uses a variety of cohesive devices and organisational patterns effectively. There is an introduction and logical development of ideas leading to concluding thoughts. The use of shorter sentences in places is appropriate for a magazine readership, encouraging the reader to continue (*'And as decades and centuries come …', 'But even if the current music taste …', 'But music still is …'*)
Language	4	There is a range of vocabulary, including less common lexis, used effectively (*'overly complex melodies paired with simple and repetitive lyrics', 'general mental well-being', 'enormously positive impact'*) and a range of both simple and complex grammatical forms is used with control and sophistication.

Listening

One mark is given for each correct answer. The total mark is converted into a score on the Cambridge English Scale for the paper.

For security reasons, several versions of the Listening paper are used at each administration of the examination. Before grading, the performance of the candidates in each of the versions is compared and marks adjusted to compensate for any imbalance in levels of difficulty.

Speaking

Candidates are assessed on their own individual performance and not in relation to each other, according to the following five analytical criteria: grammatical resource, vocabulary resource, discourse management, pronunciation and interactive communication. Assessment is based on performance in the whole test and not in particular parts of the test.

Both examiners assess the candidates. The assessor applies detailed analytical scales, and the interlocutor applies a global achievement scale, which is based on the analytical scales.

Analytical scales

Grammatical resource

This refers to the accurate and appropriate use of a range of both simple and complex forms. Performance is viewed in terms of the overall effectiveness of the language used in spoken interaction.

Vocabulary resource

This refers to the candidate's ability to use a wide range of vocabulary to meet task requirements. At Advanced level, the tasks require candidates to speculate and exchange views on unfamiliar topics. Performance is viewed in terms of the overall effectiveness of the language used in spoken interaction.

Discourse management

This refers to the candidate's ability to link utterances together to form coherent speech, without undue hesitation. The utterances should be relevant to the tasks and should be arranged logically to develop the themes or arguments required by the tasks.

Pronunciation

This refers to the candidate's ability to produce intelligible utterances to fulfil the task requirements. This includes stress and intonation as well as individual sounds. Examiners put themselves in the position of the non-ESOL specialist and assess the overall impact of the pronunciation and the degree of effort required to understand the candidate.

Interactive communication

This refers to the candidate's ability to take an active part in the development of the discourse. This requires the ability to participate in the range of interactive situations in the test and to develop discussions on a range of topics by initiating and responding appropriately. This also refers to the deployment of strategies to maintain interaction at an appropriate level throughout the test so that the tasks can be fulfilled.

Global achievement

This refers to the candidate's overall effectiveness in dealing with the tasks in the four separate parts of the Advanced Speaking test. The global mark is an independent, impression mark which reflects the assessment of the candidate's performance from the interlocutor's perspective.

Marks

Marks for each of the criteria are awarded out of a five-point scale. Marks for the Speaking test are subsequently converted into a score on the Cambridge English Scale for the paper.

Advanced typical minimum adequate performance

The candidate develops the interaction with contributions which are mostly coherent and extended when dealing with the Advanced-level tasks. Grammar is mostly accurate and vocabulary appropriate. Utterances are understood with very little strain on the listener.

Test 5 Key

Reading and Use of English (1 hour 30 minutes)

Part 1

1 C   2 A   3 A   4 B   5 C   6 B   7 D   8 B

Part 2

9 rather   10 how   11 for   12 or   13 going   14 longer   15 only   16 on

Part 3

17 unfavourable/unfavorable   18 problematic   19 intensifies   20 instability
21 effectively   22 performance   23 resistant   24 lessen

Part 4

25 parents were / are | UNAWARE of   26 as (is / it is / it's) COMMONLY | believed /
thought   27 in the MOOD | to go / for going   28 somewhere ELSE | to   29 FAILED
to realise / appreciate / understand | the significance / importance   30 there ANY |
improvement in / increase in / increase to

Part 5

31 C   32 C   33 D   34 C   35 B   36 A

Part 6

37 B   38 A   39 B   40 C

Part 7

41 F   42 B   43 D   44 G   45 E   46 C

Part 8

47 C   48 D   49 C   50 B   51 D   52 A   53 C   54 D   55 C   56 C

Writing (1 hour 30 minutes)

Candidate responses are marked using the assessment scale on pages 108–109.

Listening (approximately 40 minutes)

Part 1

1 B   2 B   3 B   4 A   5 A   6 B

Part 2

7 queen   8 colony   9 wood   10 (enough) feedback   11 staircase   12 sandbags / sand bags / bags of sand   13 intelligence   14 (mathematical) model

Part 3

15 B   16 A   17 D   18 B   19 D   20 A

Part 4

21 F   22 H   23 B   24 A   25 D   26 B   27 C   28 F   29 H   30 D

Transcript	*This is the Cambridge English Advanced Listening Test. Test Five.*
	I'm going to give you the instructions for this test.
	I'll introduce each part of the test and give you time to look at the questions.
	At the start of each piece, you'll hear this sound:
	tone
	You'll hear each piece twice.
	Remember, while you're listening, write your answers on the question paper. You'll have five minutes at the end of the test to copy your answers onto the separate answer sheet.
	There'll now be a pause. Please ask any questions now because you must not speak during the test.
	[pause]
PART 1	*Now open your question paper and look at Part One.*
	[pause]
	You'll hear three different extracts. For questions 1–6, choose the answer (A, B, or C) which fits best according to what you hear. There are two questions for each extract.
Extract One	*You hear a trainee teacher called Susanna talking to her tutor.*
	Now look at questions one and two.
	[pause]
	tone
Man:	How are you finding the teaching course, Susanna? You seem to have been making good progress so far.

Woman: Yeah, I'm feeling more confident in front of my students. But I worry about whether they're inspired by the activities I do with them sometimes. I guess this is a wake-up call for me – that it's just too much to expect them to be as excited about Maths as I am.

Man: I think when a teacher's motivated, that can't fail to make an impression. You can't expect your students to love a subject unless they can see you love it yourself. Sure, your students will think you're crazy if you talk about Maths as if it were a spectator sport, but in the end your attitude will rub off on them.

Woman: I was reading about some techniques I could try in the classroom to keep their interest levels up. I've been trying to get some more hands-on stuff into my classes – you know trying things out in a practical sense rather than sticking to boring theory.

Man: Sounds like an excellent idea. Students always appreciate a teacher who goes the extra mile for them.

[pause]

tone

[The recording is repeated.]

[pause]

Extract Two *You hear a student called Sam telling his friend Ella about a concert he's been to.*

Now look at questions three and four.

[pause]

tone

Sam: So you decided against the concert then?

Ella: I thought about it, but I don't really think it's possible to get caught up in the atmosphere when all you see is someone pressing buttons on a computer and tinkling the keys on a synthesiser. That's all this electronic music amounts to.

Sam: Admittedly the performer was dressed all in black and she looked like a scene shifter. And the visuals were limited – there was a screen, but just with some sober animations on it – trees, castles, rippling water – that sort of thing.

Ella: That says it all.

Sam: But does that matter, if the music's brilliant? And it certainly was. But that's just my opinion.

Ella: Tell me something about her then.

Sam: Well – she's a student – studying comparative literature I think. That seems to give a bit of substance to her music, make it thoughtful and rigorous.

Ella: Sounds overly serious!

Sam: Well, it all paid off. When the audience got more lively towards the end, she kept it steady and didn't change pace to build excitement. And she didn't seem to need the pyrotechnics and lasers that so many techies rely on.

[pause]

tone

[The recording is repeated.]

[pause]

Extract Three   *You hear a woman telling her friend about new policies adopted by her company.*

Now look at questions five and six.

[pause]

tone

Man: I heard that people from your office were planting trees last week. What's going on?

Woman: Sustainability's the new watchword these days. Last year we concentrated on cutting down on our use of paper, and providing raw material for more also seemed a good thing to do.

Man: And easier too – your office is next door to a big forest, isn't it?

Woman: Yes – very convenient. We're really keen on the idea that the company should be seen to identify with a certain set of values – and I think we were doing just that out there in the woods. So much internal conflict seemed forgotten too – which may not last, of course!

Man: What else have you done?

Woman: It's not just the trees of course – we've cut down our carbon footprint and reduced staff travel by encouraging remote working and flexible home working, so people have been understandably pleased about that. And word seems to have got round because the last bunch of job applicants were a very noticeably higher calibre than previously – and I'm pretty sure that wasn't just a coincidence, though it wasn't part of our original thinking. There are certainly plenty of happy clients, but they've always been keen on the idea of supporting community projects through our efforts!

[pause]

tone

[The recording is repeated.]

[pause]

That's the end of Part One.

Now turn to Part Two.

[pause]

PART 2   *You'll hear a scientist called Jim Weller giving a talk about some robots he has created and how they function like insects called termites. For questions 7–14, complete the sentences with a word or short phrase.*

You now have 45 seconds to look at Part Two.

[pause]

tone

Jim: Hi. I'm Jim, and together with colleagues I've been attempting to create a group of robots that build things in the same impressive way that termites do. Termites are like large ants and build amazingly complex structures called mounds to live in. Unlike bees, termites don't receive instructions from their queen about what to do. In fact, a single worker doesn't know what the other termites are doing or what the current overall state of the mound looks like.

This tells us that large numbers of units working independently can, paradoxically, build complicated, large-scale things together. So, we decided to make and to program what I like to call a colony of robots. Now, by giving the robots a picture of what we want them to build – and it doesn't matter how many of them there are or which robot does what – they do indeed end up building what they're asked for. The robots and termites both have very restricted sensing – a single unit can only tell what's going on right around itself. It's the same with communicating. Rather than communicating with one another directly, termites make alterations to their shared environment, and others respond. One deposits some soil, for example, or half-eaten wood … another one comes along later and on seeing this, a reaction is triggered. We observed this and devised a similar system with the robots.

Like termites, the robots often make errors, for example trying to pick up a brick and failing. Rather than trying to prevent those errors, we give them enough feedback to help with the recognition and correction process, so they try again until they get it right. So they keep patrolling the structure, fixing only what needs fixing.

I've demonstrated this in action several times in public presentations, with one of our robots. It had to try to complete the structure I asked it to, in this case a staircase. And there was a block missing at the top, so it had to try and pick up building material from the loading area and walk up the structure until it discovered exactly what needed attention.

In the long-term, one day robots like this could build for us in inaccessible or dangerous settings, such as underwater or on Mars. In the shorter term, the same principle applies. So, for instance, if you wanted to position sandbags to protect against rising floodwater, or build in difficult Antarctic surroundings, you can imagine how hardware and approaches very much like this could be used.

In a sense, termites are like cells in your brain, all acting independently but interacting with each other, and out of that comes a higher intelligence. And in a similar kind of way our robots are individuals, moving around independently with no central coordination, and together, hopefully, producing complicated structures.

One spin-off piece of research has already been put into place. A Turkish group has been working alongside us to see if the way the robots and termites operate can actually be captured in a mathematical model to be used in future projects. It's a fascinating idea and I believe there are similar studies with flocks of birds and shoals of fish. Now let me move on to …

[pause]

Now you'll hear Part Two again.

tone

[The recording is repeated.]

[pause]

That's the end of Part Two.

Now turn to Part Three.

[pause]

PART 3

You'll hear an interview in which a historian called Mark Connor and a writer called Judith Monroe are talking about the history of the underground railway in London. For questions 15–20, choose the answer (A, B, C or D) which fits best according to what you hear.

You now have 70 seconds to look at Part Three.

[pause]

tone

Interviewer: Today we are talking to historian Mark Connor and writer Judith Monroe about the history of the London Underground railway, otherwise known as the Tube, which celebrated its 150th anniversary recently. Mark, what prompted the construction of the world's first underground train system all those years ago?

Mark: Well, we tend to think that all modern problems were invented by us. But actually the 19th century also had traffic problems. Okay, it was all horse-drawn transport in those days, but still the streets were jammed. London is an old city which grew organically. It never was designed for heavy traffic and so there are lots of narrow streets. Now there was once a guy called Charles Pearson who was stuck in what we'd now call a traffic jam, and he thought of the unique solution of having a transport system that could go underground. It was a brilliant idea – but it wasn't until 30 years later that the first line was built.

Interviewer: So, Judith, how did they go about it, as an engineering project?

Judith: The first set of underground lines were built by a method called cut and cover, which was pretty crude because basically you cut open a big hole in the ground, preferably in an existing road rather than having to demolish a lot of houses – though a few houses were demolished – then you put in the railway, and covered it over again. That's a pretty disruptive form of engineering, and it did cause chaos in the centre of London for a couple of years. But amazingly, they were started in 1860 and completed by 1863. You wouldn't expect to finish a single metro line in that time these days.

125

Interviewer: And how was the first line received by the public when it finally opened, Mark?

Mark: Well, there was a big debate at first: Would people use it? Would they dare to go in it? What would they find down there? Would there be dog-sized rats and stinking sewers? I think people were quite brave, actually. The tunnels were pretty dark because they only had gas lighting at the time. In fact, on the day it opened, an incredible 30,000 people used the railway and the trains were completely full. The whole thing was profitable from year one, encouraging investors to help continue developing it.

Interviewer: And let me ask both of you, as development continued, what effect did it have?

Judith: Oh, the effects were huge. As it grew, it provided work for thousands, both in the construction and the subsequent running of the system. And it was a great source of national pride. It's hard to overestimate its importance in the way London grew – the city actually followed the spread of the underground lines, not the other way round.

Interviewer: Mark?

Mark: Don't forget London was the pioneer of this. They did it 37 years before anyone else in the world. And yes, I would say that the Underground really helped create London. The lines spread out towards what were little villages at the time – and are now important areas of the city.

Interviewer: And Judith, what about the stations?

Judith: If anyone wants to come and experience the Underground, I'd say use that extension of the Jubilee line opened in 1999. You'll see how beautiful the stations can be. They were deliberately designed as big, cavernous places with an adventurous feel of going underground, massive escalators going everywhere, a bit like the 1920s film *Metropolis* where you get the sense of being in a really huge city with lots of people going different places. A thrilling place to be. A lot of the stations on that stretch of the line are like that. They're absolutely incredible feats of engineering.

Interviewer: And what about mapping the railway? Wasn't that incredibly complicated?

Mark: Yes, what happened was, as more lines opened up, and the existing map became more complex, a guy called Harry Beck said, hang on, this map doesn't have to be geographically accurate, so he made it geographically inaccurate – just a very simple diagram – made of straight lines and 45 degree angles. I think that's one of the main ways it became something in people's heads as a system, as an icon, of London. London Underground have now made more money from the map through merchandising than they have through running trains.

[pause]

Now you'll hear Part Three again.

tone

[The recording is repeated.]

[pause]

That's the end of Part Three.

Now turn to Part Four.

[pause]

PART 4   *Part Four consists of two tasks.*

You'll hear five short extracts in which people are talking about visits they have made to museums.

Look at Task One. For questions 21–25, choose from the list (A–H) each speaker's reason for visiting the museum.

Now look at Task Two. For questions 26–30, choose from the list (A–H) what impressed each speaker most about the museum.

While you listen, you must complete both tasks.

You now have 45 seconds to look at Part Four.

[pause]

tone

Speaker One: I spent last weekend at a friend's – his parents live on the coast. He went off somewhere on Saturday leaving me struggling with the history coursework I had to finish by Monday. I wandered into the town centre and saw the museum, and I remembered how my mother always used to say that local museums are often a mine of information – and I needed inspiration. I bought my ticket from the affable guy on duty. There was plenty of material, well displayed – and a temporary exhibition of deep-sea fishing equipment – but more importantly all the stuff was closely associated with the town, and reflected its history as a once thriving fishing port.

[pause]

Speaker Two: Going to museums is not something I often do – at the moment I get enough lectures and information overload at college – but Dad's got himself a metal detector and become a treasure hunter. Last week he found this funny little brooch, and I said I'd show it to someone who'd know what it was. There were a whole lot of people there – maybe there was something special going on – and the staff kept me hanging about. So to fill the time, I tried out one of those tape machines and listened to a lively commentary which certainly made the displays and reconstructions more relevant. I didn't come back with any good news for Dad though. No treasure this time!

[pause]

Speaker Three: I've got a German friend staying at the moment, and last week I dragged him off to the town museum – I thought he might learn a bit of local history. A team of archaeologists have been working in the town-centre car park and unearthed an unusual bit of prehistoric pottery. It's in the museum for now, and I was very keen to take a look and see what the experts were saying about it. My friend said he'd bring his new camera. The hoard has already been researched in detail, and the staff have produced an in-depth explanatory leaflet reflecting this – I was really pleased to learn so much and my friend was pretty chuffed at how his new camera performed.

[pause]

Speaker Four: I remember going to our local museum when I was in primary school – it was very boring – but I hadn't been back again until last week. I was really surprised to find they'd made several changes. They have those audio-guides now and weekly lectures, and the information boards have been updated. And to crown it all – instead of having everything in cabinets, they've built mock-up scenes – like a mediaeval kitchen for example – convincingly realistic and much more effective. I managed to do some half-decent sketches of them – a friend in the States studying the period had asked me to do this for him. There were a lot of people – I'm not surprised the place is more popular these days.

[pause]

Speaker Five: I was away on a course last week. We were kept busy – lectures all day, plenty of reading to catch up on in the evenings. I did manage to visit the local industrial museum at the instigation of a colleague who thought I'd find it interesting, 'cos it was full of examples of nineteenth-century machinery, which you could get right up to. There were galleries full of huge, gleaming marvels of engineering. To be honest, the machines looked much the same and the vast amounts of technical information went straight over my head, though this was obviously a source of frustration for all the enthusiasts who seemed to come from everywhere, judging by the amazing number of different languages I heard.

[pause]

Now you'll hear Part Four again.

tone

[The recording is repeated.]

[pause]

That's the end of Part Four.

There'll now be a pause of five minutes for you to copy your answers onto the separate answer sheet. Be sure to follow the numbering of all the questions. I'll remind you when there's one minute left, so that you're sure to finish in time.

[Teacher, pause the recording here for five minutes. Remind students when they have one minute left.]

That's the end of the test. Please stop now. Your supervisor will now collect all the question papers and answer sheets.

Test 6 Key

Reading and Use of English (1 hour 30 minutes)

Part 1

1 C   2 D   3 B   4 C   5 D   6 C   7 B   8 D

Part 2

9 from / with   10 which   11 their   12 do   13 as   14 bring   15 must / should
16 it / this

Part 3

17 inhabited   18 height   19 descendant   20 mountainous   21 Findings
22 originated   23 adaptations   24 storage

Part 4

25 as SOON as | we have received / we receive   26 hadn't / had not | put UP   27 delay |
was / had been CAUSED by the   28 it hadn't / had not been | FOR Sarah's; it wasn't /
was not / weren't / were not | FOR Sarah's   29 with the EXCEPTION of Leo | came
30 was DUE | to start / begin

Part 5

31 B   32 A   33 B   34 A   35 A   36 A

Part 6

37 A   38 D   39 C   40 D

Part 7

41 G   42 B   43 D   44 C   45 E   46 F

Part 8

47 C   48 D   49 B   50 A   51 D   52 C   53 A   54 D   55 B   56 C

Writing (1 hour 30 minutes)

Candidate responses are marked using the assessment scale on pages 108–109.

Listening (approximately 40 minutes)

Part 1

1 A   2 C   3 B   4 A   5 C   6 A

Part 2

7 popular   **8** insect   **9** green gold   **10** (the) storms   **11** nets / netting
12 (small) holes   **13** boiled   **14** blankets

Part 3

15 D   16 A   17 B   18 A   19 C   20 D

Part 4

21 H   22 A   23 F   24 E   25 C   26 D   27 B   28 G   29 A   30 H

Transcript	*This is the Cambridge English Advanced Listening Test. Test Six.*
	I'm going to give you the instructions for this test.
	I'll introduce each part of the test and give you time to look at the questions.
	At the start of each piece you'll hear this sound:
	tone
	You'll hear each piece twice.
	Remember, while you're listening, write your answers on the question paper. You'll have five minutes at the end of the test to copy your answers onto the separate answer sheet.
	There'll now be a pause. Please ask any questions now because you must not speak during the test.
	[pause]
PART 1	*Now open your question paper and look at Part One.*
	[pause]
	You'll hear three different extracts. For questions 1–6, choose the answer (A, B, or C) which fits best according to what you hear. There are two questions for each extract.
Extract One	*You hear a sportsman and a businesswoman discussing the issue of being competitive.*
	Now look at questions one and two.
	[pause]
	tone

Woman: You've read this new book on competitiveness. Is it all about striving for success, or a defence of the Olympic ideal? You know – taking part is more important than winning.

Man: Well, yes, that's a view often ridiculed certainly, as some sort of excuse for underachievement. I mean if you run a race, surely it's because you want to win, and we've all got used to the belief that competition is a necessary force for good in the modern world. It's a deeply ingrained idea. It was a bit of a shock to read that competition impoverishes people rather than enriching them. There's the mind-boggling range of convincing examples you'd expect in support of this theory, and the whole thing is so engagingly written that the most hostile opponents would have trouble refuting it.

Woman: Well my experience of competition in the business world is nothing but negative. I'd say that if you put competition at the heart of your strategy, far from achieving the desired outcome of boosting efficiency by pitting staff against each other, the effect is rather to encourage people to focus exclusively on immediate success … not on sustained growth. Let's face it, the best businesses are the ones that look ahead instead of limiting their perspective in this way.

[pause]

tone

[The recording is repeated.]

[pause]

Extract Two   *You hear two friends discussing some research into the impact of colour on memory. Now look at questions three and four.*

[pause]

tone

Woman: You know how colours affect us, like red and yellow are often used in fast food restaurants … in the décor I mean.

Man: Yeah, yeah – they say they excite the brain, which tells you you're hungry – that was in the papers years back.

Woman: Well, OK, but now there's a suggestion colours may help us memorise better.

Man: Oh, come on. Influence appetites and emotions, maybe, but …

Woman: No, really – this teenager did some research.

Man: Teenager?

Woman: Yeah I know – but it does seem sound. She took a page of words and printed them in so-called 'warm colours' …

Man: How do you mean?

Woman: Well, reds, oranges, yellows, etc. – and gave people two minutes to memorise the words. She followed that with pretty complicated maths equations to stop them reciting the words in their head.

Man:	Hmm … OK, sounds good so far …
Woman:	And they were given a minute to record how many words they could remember. And then the same procedure with words printed in cool colours like green and blue.
Man:	And?
Woman:	Overall warm colours were memorised better and cool colours worse.
Man:	She's followed a thorough process, then. But is there any existing published data that backs up or contradicts these claims?
Woman:	Well, not as such, I grant you. Though it sounds like she's onto something to me. But only time will tell.
Man:	Hmm …

[pause]

tone

[The recording is repeated.]

[pause]

Extract Three	*You hear two people discussing a television programme about music and the effect it has on the brain.*
	Now look at questions five and six.

[pause]

tone

Woman:	I watched '*How Musical are you?*' on TV last night – they were saying how listening to music is a really complicated process. The scientists were really going to town on it!
Man:	I thought so-called musicality meant being able to play a musical instrument, but that seemed to be just one aspect of the whole programme. It's odd, people who've never set foot inside a music classroom might still have a musical 'ear' without realising it!
Woman:	You mean, everyone has an innate ability to make sense of music? I'm not sure but it brings an enormous amount of pleasure. I really don't know how, but it changes my mood when I'm down – which never ceases to amaze me! But they missed a trick in not clarifying why some people are avid listeners to music and others not.
Man:	They seemed more interested in the possible effect of music on musicians' brains. I didn't know that people who've had music training in childhood find long-term positive effects on their verbal memory – who'd have thought it.
Woman:	I don't remember words whatever I do! You know that on-line quiz they mentioned – that might be worth a go. It's about how engaged you are with music, you know, whether it's part of your identity or not.
Man:	So you might be more musical than you think!

[pause]

tone

[The recording is repeated.]

[pause]

That's the end of Part One.

Now turn to Part Two.

[pause]

PART 2   *You'll hear a radio report by the journalist Susie Stubbs, who has been to the tropical island of Réunion to find out about the flavouring called vanilla. For questions 7–14, complete the sentences with a word or short phrase. You now have 45 seconds to look at Part Two.*

[pause]

tone

Susie: This week's edition of World Farming comes from the island of Réunion, off the south-east coast of Africa, where there are vanilla plantations as far as the eye can see. Vanilla is an exotic spice which is very nearly the most expensive in the world – second only to saffron – and certainly the most popular. We're used to tasting it in sweet dishes, but people are now beginning to use it in savoury ones as well. In fact, there's a restaurant near where I live in London, called Fresh Tastes, where chef Antonio Meltini adds vanilla to almost all the dishes, and quite delicious they are too!

These days vanilla is grown in the Caribbean, East Asia and Africa, but it originated in Mexico, where there is a particular insect which can pollinate the plant. This morning, I visited a vanilla plantation here on Réunion. I heard local people referring to the plants as 'green gold' – which isn't surprising when you think of all the money they represent. Good vanilla is always in great demand and the price at the moment is between £150 and £180 a kilo for top quality. In fact there's been a problem with supplying customers recently, as storms have had a detrimental effect on the harvest – all the more unfortunate, now the various diseases which used to decimate the crop have been eradicated.

I'm told that some of the earlier producers had their vanilla growing in the shelter of trees, but on modern plantations the plants are grown under nets, which can easily be removed when it's time to harvest the vanilla seed pods, which are the valuable part of the plant. After three or four years of growth the first flowers appear, but they only bloom for a day – they need to be pollinated then, either naturally or artificially. Later on, the pods – they're a kind of shell or case which holds the seeds – are harvested. The pickers often make small holes at one end of the pods, as a means of identifying their farm or plantation. Any pods with black marks on them will probably be rejected at this stage. Healthy-looking pods are dried outside in the sun, then they are boiled for about three minutes – which surprised me rather – but if this isn't done, the pods will open and all the seeds will be lost. So it's a very important part of the process. Then the pods are put in boxes which have blankets wrapped round them to retain the heat. Materials like polystyrene have been experimented with, and found unsatisfactory apparently. Finally, when the pods have dried out enough, they're put into new boxes, to allow their characteristic aroma to develop.

I was allowed to open up one of these boxes – they're really just like treasure chests. The fragrance is wonderfully …

[pause]

Now you'll hear Part Two again.

tone

[The recording is repeated.]

[pause]

That's the end of Part Two.

Now turn to Part Three.

[pause]

PART 3 *You'll hear a radio interview in which two young journalists called Angus Brown and Yolanda Zouche are talking about their work.*

For questions 15–20, choose the answer (A, B, C or D) which fits best according to what you hear.

You now have 70 seconds to look at Part Three.

[pause]

tone

Interviewer: Today I'm talking to two young journalists – Angus Brown, a news reporter on a national daily, and Yolanda Zouche, a features writer on a London evening paper. You're both not only successful in your careers, but enthusiastic about them too. What would you say is the most challenging aspect of your work. Yolanda?

Yolanda: I'm tempted to say nothing really – I like it all, some things more, some less. Our features are a mix of things that have been thought of and researched and written in advance, and more urgent, topical pieces with a quick turnaround. I'm sometimes sent out on a story that's needed for the next day. It's pretty scary when you know you've got just a few hours – and it can involve finding people whose addresses you don't know. That's the same with any story, of course. You'll have to think up ideas for pictures to go with it and, write your piece to a fixed word count – but you soon find yourself doing this automatically.

Interviewer: And what do you both enjoy about your work?

Yolanda: Well, I suppose I'm quite a nosy kind of person, so I love digging out stories that haven't been reported – I'll go from interviewing a singer about a forthcoming tour to investigating some crime, all in one day perhaps. I'd be bored otherwise, I think, and then it's all got to be presented in a way that will make people want to read it.

Interviewer: And you, Angus?

Angus: There's no way I could describe 'my typical working day' – that's the sort of question people often ask. And that's really why I enjoy it so much I suppose – so many fascinating people to talk to, and so much to learn.

Interviewer: Like several other papers nowadays, Angus, yours has an online version. What do you think is the greatest significance of the change to digital?

Angus: It's completely altered the way we think about the news. Things move so very quickly, and we really do need to stay receptive to all the opportunities the medium has opened up. I think maybe more people are better informed these days. We've certainly become a rolling news operation – I can now file a story as soon as it breaks, early and then update digitally as I find out more. And if I get anything wrong, people are all too quick to point this out on social media.

Interviewer: Finding a job is not easy for anyone – what was it like for you Angus?

Angus: It certainly wasn't easy. People continually told me that print journalism was dead, and there was no money in it, but in fact I had to beat 1,800 applicants to get on the graduate scheme. Before that I'd been on a couple of temporary work experience placements with a local paper – you can do these to get a taster of the work, but there's no salary … I managed financially because I was doing some part-time teaching at the same time. You really need some sort of support network of people with influence too – luckily the work experience provided that.

Interviewer: Tell us what qualities you think a would-be journalist needs, Yolanda.

Yolanda: There's no straightforward answer to that – I've got an English degree and Angus is a historian, I believe … that's his academic background. There are plenty of good courses around, and eventually you'll have to get to grips with some of the technical stuff – like media law, and so on. But remember no one is ever going to employ a shy retiring type with no ideas. Being able to write clearly and quickly, and think through a tangle of information is obviously helpful – but these are things you can develop with practice.

Interviewer: And what would you say, Angus, is a good preparation for an aspiring journalist?

Angus: I'm wary of long periods of unpaid work experience – you can easily end up doing someone else's job for free, but some is pretty well essential. Listen to people's conversations. It's a great way to get ideas for stories – everything you see and hear is copy for articles. Being a good writer is obviously an advantage as I've said, but it's more important to have something to write about. You don't need to be, and probably won't ever become, an expert in anything, but you'll have the chance to engage with a huge variety of different issues and topics.

Interviewer: Thank you both for sharing your ideas and experience.

[pause]

Now you'll hear Part Three again.

tone

[The recording is repeated.]

[pause]

That's the end of Part Three.

Now turn to Part Four.

[pause]

PART 4

Part Four consists of two tasks.

You'll hear five short extracts in which people are talking about strategies they've adopted for handling work-related problems.

Look at Task One. For questions 21–25, choose from the list (A–H) why each speaker decided to adopt their particular strategy.

Now look at Task Two. For questions 26–30, choose from the list (A–H) how each speaker felt after implementing the strategy.

While you listen, you must complete both tasks.

You now have 45 seconds to look at Part Four.

[pause]

tone

Speaker One: Having a part in a long-running play might seem glamorous but there are drawbacks. My fellow actors and I share pretty cramped accommodation, for one thing – tolerance can be stretched to the limit. But I was determined to create my own hideaway, somewhere I could escape to and read quietly, so I squirreled myself away in a hidden corner under the stage only to find two other fresh-faced cast members already there, thoroughly at home, drinking tea. We looked at each other in stunned silence – then giggled uncontrollably. What else could we do? Now we gather there before every performance for a bit of quiet, so there's a strict no talking rule!

[pause]

Speaker Two: A hospital doctor's life isn't the easiest, but I love my job. A couple of months ago though, I made a drastic decision – I changed hospital, so now my commute is just a 12-minute walk from home. I hadn't foreseen how much more involved in the local community I'd become thanks to swapping my daily drive for a brisk walk – knowing local shopkeepers by name and so on. I can't get enough of it. And it means I can play with my three-year-old son at both ends of the day, which let's face it is what drove me to act in the first place. It compensates enormously for the stress and long hours.

[pause]

Speaker Three: I've been the manager at several football clubs, and it doesn't get any easier. The work itself is varied and complicated, but it's the garbage the media comes up with that really gets on my nerves. Half of it's invented, and on occasion it impacts on my kids and friends too, which makes my blood boil.

So two seasons ago, I implemented a self-imposed ban – I won't go on social media or message boards, or read newspaper articles. That's why I hadn't a clue why the players were applauding me into the dressing room one morning – turned out they'd seen a press photograph of me doing my charity work at a local school the weekend before.

[pause]

Speaker Four: Working as a TV presenter, live on air, brings its own set of challenges. To be honest I never quite know what's going to happen, even now. The system I drew up after the first couple of hectic shows – having a number of back-up plans – was aimed at helping the situation but I confess I still regularly tear my hair out at producers forgetting to tell me of last minute changes to the guest list. It throws my elaborate system into complete disarray. I try to bear in mind however, that there's another show tomorrow, and the day after – there's no point getting too worked up.

[pause]

Speaker Five: As school principal, I'm very conscious of how many people are in my care – not only students and teachers but also ancillary staff and, indirectly, parents. I need to have my act together, which means getting to work early, and am often the last to leave. So last year I hit on the idea of going running – fifteen kilometres, three nights a week. I'd give anything to swap my slow and clumsy running style with the streamlined joggers gliding effortlessly past me, but as hoped, I'm finding that if there's something I need to deal with in school, I can usually find a solution while running, and arrive home relaxed – much to my wife's relief.

[pause]

Now you'll hear Part Four again.

tone

[The recording is repeated.]

[pause]

That's the end of Part Four.

There'll now be a pause of five minutes for you to copy your answers onto the separate answer sheet. Be sure to follow the numbering of all the questions. I'll remind you when there's one minute left, so that you're sure to finish in time.

[Teacher, pause the recording here for five minutes. Remind students when they have one minute left.]

That's the end of the test. Please stop now. Your supervisor will now collect all the question papers and answer sheets.

Test 7 Key

Reading and Use of English (1 hour 30 minutes)

Part 1

1 A   2 D   3 D   4 B   5 C   6 A   7 D   8 B

Part 2

9 why   10 but / except / besides   11 like   12 does   13 my   14 on   15 despite
16 otherwise

Part 3

17 endurance   18 doubtless / undoubtedly   19 tolerant   20 massive   21 usefulness
22 accessible   23 anxieties   24 hopefully

Part 4

25 to include / mention / leave in / use | ANY of   26 was sorry (that) | he COULD not
27 lost | SIGHT of   28 no MATTER | how hard I   29 comes ACROSS | to his boss as
30 made no | REFERENCE to; didn't / did not make (any / a) | REFERENCE to

Part 5

31 C   32 C   33 D   34 B   35 B   36 C

Part 6

37 D   38 D   39 A   40 C

Part 7

41 C   42 G   43 D   44 F   45 A   46 E

Part 8

47 C   48 B   49 D   50 C   51 A   52 B   53 D   54 B   55 C   56 B

Writing (1 hour 30 minutes)

Candidate responses are marked using the assessment scale on pages 108–109.

Listening (approximately 40 minutes)

Part 1

1 C   2 C   3 A   4 C   5 A   6 C

Part 2

7 Water Response   8 light bulbs   9 (chemical) sponge   10 reproductive   11 wave action / waves / (the) action of the waves   12 (the) land   13 lemon juice / lemons   14 oil leaks / oil leaking

Part 3

15 A   16 D   17 C   18 D   19 B   20 A

Part 4

21 G   22 H   23 D   24 F   25 E   26 H   27 D   28 C   29 B   30 G

Transcript	*This is the Cambridge English Advanced Listening Test. Test Seven.*
	I'm going to give you the instructions for this test.
	I'll introduce each part of the test and give you time to look at the questions.
	At the start of each piece you'll hear this sound:
	tone
	You'll hear each piece twice.
	Remember, while you're listening, write your answers on the question paper. You'll have five minutes at the end of the test to copy your answers onto the separate answer sheet.
	There'll now be a pause. Please ask any questions now, because you must not speak during the test.
	[pause]
PART 1	*Now open your question paper and look at Part One.*
	[pause]
	You'll hear three different extracts. For questions 1–6, choose the answer (A, B, or C) which fits best according to what you hear. There are two questions for each extract.
Extract One	*You hear two friends talking about online privacy. Now look at questions one and two.*
	[pause]
	tone

Man:	You know, I think privacy as we used to understand it is a thing of the past.
Woman:	Why do you say that? Not another scare story in the papers? They're always full of fanciful tales of doom and gloom …
Man:	You may laugh, but after what happened yesterday …
Woman:	What did happen?
Man:	I was discussing the whole issue with an uncle of mine, who's just turned 85. He proudly informed me there couldn't be any data relating to him on the internet because he'd never used a computer.
Woman:	Well fair enough, surely?
Man:	Well, I only spent a couple of minutes searching and was still able to come up with quite a bit of stuff about him.
Woman:	Really? That's a bit worrying. I bet he was taken aback, wasn't he?
Man:	He was stunned … speechless – asked me to remove it all from 'cyberspace'. But it doesn't work like that, of course. What's there, is there.
Woman:	That does seem an erosion of privacy. Mind you, come to think of it, I suppose there's also been some information available on us all for a while, way before the days of the internet.
Man:	But it wasn't so easy to get at. And the situation's not going to improve.
Woman:	No … I guess not. Quite the opposite.
	[pause]
	tone
	[The recording is repeated.]
	[pause]

Extract Two	*You hear two trainee chefs discussing the issue of food waste. Now look at questions three and four.*
	[pause]
	tone
Woman:	Did you know that over seven million tonnes of food is thrown away every year in the UK?
Man:	Really? That's one big garbage mountain.
Woman:	Yeah – and it costs huge amounts to collect, not to mention clogging landfills and producing vast amounts of CO_2 emissions.
Man:	There's not much we can do about it though, is there?
Woman:	Well actually, restaurants are some of the worst offenders. That's why we adopted responsible practices in our kitchen a while back. We've only got one garbage bin now despite having 100 seats, but two compost machines for food waste.
Man:	Oh come on! We've got four or five bins and only 60 seats at our place.

Woman: Look, anything is possible. Our place is unrecognisable from what it was like last year, as is my boss – can't think what's got into him! Thinking ahead for a change!

Man: Hmmm. OK – maybe I'd better talk to my head chef. Might be fighting an uphill battle though.

Woman: There're other things you can do too – my chef's obsessive about portion control, keeping an eye on how much food customers leave, and altering dishes accordingly.

Man: Don't you get complaints about small servings?

Woman: Granted, we don't do enormous portions – but if occasionally someone wants a little bit more, we'll give it to them. It works – honest!

Man: Don't suppose we'd go far down that road.

[pause]

tone

[The recording is repeated.]

[pause]

Extract Three   *You hear two students talking about an experiment into the way people perceive time.*

Now look at questions five and six.

[pause]

tone

Man: Do you know anything about that experiment the lecturer was referring to?

Woman: I've looked it up – it involved this Frenchman spending two months in a cave under a glacier – in 1962 I think it was. He was 100m below ground, and because he had nothing to track the time – no clock obviously, no sun either – he got disorientated. When he came back up, he thought he'd been down there for just 34 days. Very revealing for the researchers, who'd anticipated it would go the other way. Various stuntmen and entertainers have done similar things to push themselves to extremes – but then of course they've always got an eye on the headlines they'll create.

Man: That's fascinating.

Woman: Yes, it's all about temporal landmarks – they're really important. If you build more of them into your life, you'll experience time differently. Days and years won't be one undifferentiated mush. Temporal landmarks help stop the feeling that time's whizzing by. I bet, for example, you retain memories of events that happen near the beginning or end of term – they're kind of landmarks – better than those that happened somewhere in between.

Man: So?

Woman: So establish a few landmarks – remember to mark special events like birthdays properly with some sort of celebration.

Man: That's advice I'm happy to follow.

[pause]

tone

[The recording is repeated.]

[pause]

That's the end of Part One.

Now turn to Part Two.

[pause]

PART 2   *You'll hear a woman called Sarah Harvey talking about her work with an environmental organisation which helps to protect the seas from pollution.*

For questions 7–14, complete the sentences with a word or short phrase.

You now have 45 seconds to look at Part Two.

[pause]

tone

Sarah: Welcome to my talk about my work to protect the oceans from the growing problem of pollution. I think many people are unaware of just how serious this is and the consequences it has for marine life. My interest started when I was working as a volunteer on a beach clean-up project called 'Cleaner coasts' and was introduced to my current boss. He persuaded me to come and work full-time for the environmental group he'd just established under the name 'Water Response', and I've never regretted my decision.

I soon found myself face-to-face with the direct consequences of ocean pollution, as my job involves helping to save seabirds who've swallowed the litter found floating on ocean surfaces, mistaking it for food. There is such a wide range of garbage entering the oceans now, and we rescue birds that've consumed everything from plastic bags to balloons, and even light bulbs on occasion, would you believe. Things like plastic bottle tops are common finds, unfortunately, too. Another aspect of my work is removing as much of this debris from the coast as possible.

Plastics are particularly dangerous for marine creatures as they contain what are known as organic pollutants. This is because plastics draw in a high concentration of damaging poisons, acting like a sort of chemical sponge. This is really bad news you see. These chemicals affect not only a seabird's digestive system, which is to be expected, but, what was news to me was that they also damage its reproductive system. I was well aware that toxins are also notoriously harmful to the immune system, making it harder for many marine species to fight disease.

Another problem with plastic is its durability – it doesn't go away like natural materials do, but just goes from being, say, a floating bottle to tiny plastic particles, attractive to marine creatures. This results from the action of sunlight, but wave action also plays a part in the fragmentation process.

Unfortunately, ocean pollution is increasing, despite various international conventions set up to control it. Around 100 million tonnes of plastic are produced annually, of which a shocking ten million tonnes end up in the sea. The majority of this gets there from land sources, although marine sources are actually responsible for dumping as much as 3.5 million tonnes of plastic each year.

As well as removing debris and caring for marine animals, I'm also involved in raising public awareness of the problem. I help run educational projects teaching people how to make small changes in their daily lives, like avoiding chemical-based detergents which can get into waterways and eventually find their way into the sea. I encourage others to try simple ingredients such as lemon juice for various household chores instead of their regular cleaning product. This can be remarkably effective. Even things like keeping cars well-maintained is essential for ocean protection because oil leaks get washed down drains and end up causing more pollution than the car tyres you see abandoned on beaches. Irresponsible though tyre dumping is, we've at least got a chance of stopping the tyres from getting into the sea.

Well, I want to show you a video now of our staff …

[pause]

Now you'll hear Part Two again.

tone

[The recording is repeated.]

[pause]

That's the end of Part Two.

Now turn to Part Three.

[pause]

PART 3   *You'll hear a radio interview in which two web designers called Rob Thorn and Sophie Unwin are discussing aspects of their work.*

For questions 15–20, choose the answer (A, B, C or D) which fits best according to what you hear.

You now have 70 seconds to look at Part Three.

[pause]

tone

Interviewer: With me today are two website designers, Rob Thorn, who works freelance and Sophie Unwin, a company employee, who are going to tell us something about their work. Sophie, how does what you do compare with the work of designers who deal with physical materials?

Sophie: Well, I think for all designers the key thing is enthusiasm for what you're doing. People talk about the constraints of technology, but technology is after all simply the medium we work with. It just happens to be a medium that changes all the time. As someone once said, 'The digital train waits for

143

no one; once you get off, it's very hard to catch up again.' And as in any field of design, even web design, what you create needs to be something beautiful, but perhaps more importantly, it needs to be functional.

Interviewer: So Sophie what are the critical elements of a successful web design in your view?

Sophie: It's best to remember that as far as clients are concerned, a website is good or bad depending on how much business it generates – they're not overly concerned with how pretty it looks. So that's a message for designers who pride themselves on pixel perfect detail! A website that's just like so many others won't attract much attention – but anything really wacky and off-the-wall can be nearly as bad. The core of the design though is layout – is it easy to find your way around and track down what you want to know? The way the information is illustrated often contributes to this.

Interviewer: I can see you nodding in agreement Rob. Website design clearly covers many disciplines – how did you first get involved?

Rob: Computers have fascinated me since I was a kid – I started learning C plus plus – my first computer language – when I was 13 and my dream was to be a game developer. After a few years I could do simple games, but then the internet really took off and I got interested in websites. I learnt some more languages, and could see it was going to be easier to sell a website than a game. So I got started on graphics – which I needed for my web projects – but I soon found I was better at designing than writing code.

Interviewer: Sophie – you started out as a freelancer, but have now joined a company. How has that worked out for you?

Sophie: Well, as a freelancer I had to spend a lot more of my time with clients, and even though a typical freelance business is small, it still requires a degree of paperwork. And there were always odd things cropping up with that – things I hadn't foreseen. That can be unsettling. The main difference is I now spend 80% of my time designing and coding – which I love doing and where I feel confident. I must say though that as a freelancer the feeling of entrepreneurship, the freedom and the sense of responsibility was something I relished.

Interviewer: Rob – you're a freelancer who has that sort of freedom. Tell us something about your relationship with clients.

Rob: First off of course you've got to convince a client you're an established professional, someone who turns up on time for meetings, but you also need to be the friendly guy he can trust. You need to trust him too – I've found those who start out with a whole lot of questions about money may well have problems paying. I prefer to tell them I'll get something done in say two weeks and surprise them by doing it in ten days, rather than promising five days and missing the deadline. As for clients – and there are plenty – who have no design experience but do have crazily impractical ideas – I don't fight them, just back my decisions with sound argument.

Interviewer: Finally, a question for both of you – where does your inspiration come from? You first Sophie …

Sophie: I'd say anywhere and everywhere! If you can train yourself to get in the right frame of mind, a cloud in the sky or rainwater in a puddle can spark an idea. I do quite a lot of drawing and sometimes use my sketches in new projects. And I make sure I know what other designers are doing.

Rob: And there are certainly some brilliant ones around! Sophie talked earlier about rapid technological advances – it's an absolute must to know what's going on, but it's a means to an end. But inspiration – I think it's the way you look at what's around you, not what you look at, that counts.

[pause]

Now you'll hear Part Three again.

tone

[The recording is repeated.]

[pause]

That's the end of Part Three.

Now turn to Part Four.

[pause]

PART 4 *Part Four consists of two tasks.*

You'll hear five short extracts in which people are talking about spending time working on a magazine.

Look at Task One. For questions 21–25, choose from the list (A–H) the benefit each speaker gained from the experience of working on a magazine.

Now look at Task Two. For questions 26–30, choose from the list (A–H) the personal quality each speaker thinks is most important for magazine work.

While you listen, you must complete both tasks.

You now have 45 seconds to look at Part Four.

[pause]

tone

Speaker One: I'm studying journalism at university, so when the chance of a summer job at Wow! magazine came up, I jumped at it. It was unpaid, but it was totally worth the effort. I learned more about the trade in six weeks on the magazine than I did in two years at college! I did a lot of overtime – I was exhausted by the end of the day – but I was keen, so I didn't mind. In fact, it's vital to go the extra mile – it gets you noticed, and makes it more likely that you'll be offered a job when you've finally graduated.

[pause]

Speaker Two: I think, to make it in the magazine business, you have to be a certain type of person. I mean, I'm quite sociable, which is fine – but I'm not what you'd call pushy. I'll do what's asked of me – whether it's checking computer records or even working extra hours – because I don't want to cause a fuss. But the people I met in the office were all very driven. They knew what they wanted and would go to any lengths to get their way. I think that's essential in journalism, and this realisation has kind of put me off it, frankly. It's not really me. Time to explore other options.

145

[pause]

Speaker Three: I was surprised to get a temporary job at *Country House* magazine. The staff weren't at all as I'd expected – everyone was so friendly and welcoming. That was a relief because I'm quite shy, and get nervous when I meet new people. I did mostly administrative work. I'm good at that sort of thing – I can apply myself to any task – so I made a good impression. The editor told me she liked people with focus – they make the best journalists. And I met some interesting people who promised to help me find work when I finally graduate, if I decide to go into journalism – so that was nice.

[pause]

Speaker Four: A friend of my Uncle got me a job on the magazine. It wasn't badly paid, and the hours were decent. The thing was, though, everyone seemed so fussy and obsessed with little things – like they'd go mad if I got a date wrong, or misspelt someone's name. I guess that kind of nit-picking is a must for journalists though, especially with an online magazine. Anyway, my worry was, I knew I wasn't really much of a team player – I preferred to do my own thing – but I was prepared to put that to one side and try and knuckle down and take orders, which produced good results.

[pause]

Speaker Five: I'm quite a precise sort of person, but I'm not afraid of saying what I think or pushing boundaries. Turns out they quite liked those qualities at the magazine. That's one thing I would say – you have to be creative and come up with original ideas if you're to climb the ladder in this profession. You can't afford to take it easy! That said, the rewards are worth it. The feeling I got when my first story appeared in that week's edition – what a buzz to see my name in print! I can see how journalists get hooked on it. I'm glad I did it – now I can't wait to get qualified.

[pause]

Now you'll hear Part Four again.

tone

[The recording is repeated.]

[pause]

That's the end of Part Four.

There'll now be a pause of five minutes for you to copy your answers onto the separate answer sheet. Be sure to follow the numbering of all the questions. I'll remind you when there's one minute left, so that you're sure to finish in time.

[Teacher, pause the recording here for five minutes. Remind students when they have one minute left.]

That's the end of the test. Please stop now. Your supervisor will now collect all the question papers and answer sheets.

Test 8 Key

Reading and Use of English (1 hour 30 minutes)

Part 1

1 D   2 A   3 B   4 A   5 D   6 C   7 B   8 D

Part 2

9 did / walked   10 between   11 are   12 majority   13 a / one   14 with   15 order
16 to

Part 3

17 reliance   18 awesome   19 significant   20 relation   21 considerably
22 substantial   23 annoyance   24 dismissive

Part 4

25 has / is NOTHING | to do   26 NOTIFY you of / about | any changes; NOTIFY you if
there are | changes   27 have TAKEN | our / more time   28 his doctor's ADVICE | David
cut; ADVICE from his doctor | David cut   29 to hear | a MORE   30 sooner HAD | the job
(vacancy) been; sooner HAD | the company's vacancy been

Part 5

31 D   32 A   33 A   34 B   35 D   36 B

Part 6

37 C   38 D   39 C   40 B

Part 7

41 E   42 C   43 B   44 G   45 D   46 F

Part 8

47 B   48 C   49 B   50 D   51 C   52 C   53 B   54 A   55 D   56 C

Writing (1 hour 30 minutes)

Candidate responses are marked using the assessment scale on pages 108–109.

Listening (approximately 40 minutes)

Part 1

1 B   2 A   3 B   4 B   5 B   6 A

Part 2

7 chemist   8 bubbles   9 problematic   10 drying   11 marketing   12 packaging
13 vegetarians   14 initiative

Part 3

15 D   16 D   17 B   18 A   19 C   20 C

Part 4

21 B   22 G   23 F   24 E   25 H   26 A   27 H   28 G   29 C   30 E

Transcript

This is the Cambridge English Advanced Listening Test. Test Eight.

I'm going to give you the instructions for this test.

I'll introduce each part of the test and give you time to look at the questions.

At the start of each piece you'll hear this sound:

tone

You'll hear each piece twice.

Remember, while you're listening, write your answers on the question paper. You'll have five minutes at the end of the test to copy your answers onto the separate answer sheet.

There'll now be a pause. Please ask any questions now, because you must not speak during the test.

[pause]

PART 1

Now open your question paper and look at Part One.

[pause]

You'll hear three different extracts. For questions 1–6, choose the answer (A, B, or C) which fits best according to what you hear. There are two questions for each extract.

Extract One

You hear part of a radio interview with a product designer called Charles Loughlan. Now look at questions one and two.

[pause]

tone

Interviewer: Charles, you're retired now, but you actually designed some 600 household products, and all of them as an employee of a company. Did it ever frustrate you that you were making products without your name on?

Charles: It was standard practice. Besides, I needed a weekly pay check before I needed recognition. Nowadays, you can find designers' names on products, but it tends to be high-profile people seeking attention. And then there's celebrity endorsement and all that. People think that if they buy a soccer ball that has the name of some famous player on it, they're going to score wonderful goals … a ploy to get you to buy products.

Interviewer: What advice do you have for young designers?

Charles: What they do will affect so many people during the lifetime of that product. That's serious stuff. So the product should do what it's supposed to do and be pleasing to have in your environment. I tried to make things appear as if they just belong. They don't need to scream. I don't think a nutcracker needs to look like an elephant.

[pause]

tone

[The recording is repeated.]

[pause]

Extract Two   *You hear two friends discussing a TV interview with an actress called Celia Dent. Now look at questions three and four.*

[pause]

tone

Man: Well, what a one-sided interview *that* was – and with one of my favourite actresses. She hardly got a look-in! No-one would've learned anything new about her, especially as it was the usual, tired stuff being put to her. When she did try to steer things in a different direction, the interviewer just ignored her and kept going on about himself.

Woman: There aren't many really good interviewers, are there? The best ones really take on board what's being said and follow it up. This guy showed no imagination at all, just covering old ground, and targeting obvious stuff. No wonder he couldn't get interesting responses.

Man: And Celia could've told a few stories … she's had a fascinating life. I know some film actors are perhaps a bit tricky – some seem afraid to be themselves, like they're desperate to keep up their public image at all costs. And of course many actors are interviewed just after their last film's been released, and are understandably keen to publicise it, but interviewers often concentrate on other superficial stuff. I love it when actors are challenged a bit, and the interviewer dares to deviate from the set script, putting them on the spot!

[pause]

tone

[The recording is repeated.]

[pause]

Extract Three	*You hear two freelance journalists talking about their work. Now look at questions five and six.*

[pause]

tone

Man: Hmm, I must get down to some work.

Woman: Is getting started tricky for you?

Man: Well, it can take me a while to enter into a creative state, but once I'm there, I lose awareness of absolutely anything but the ideas flowing – don't even perceive my fingers typing.

Woman: Really?

Man: Mm, and I'm then extremely resistant to interruption, so I'll shout at anyone who knocks at my study door. My defensive reactions are subconscious, though, and usually I don't even recall them. The family's used to it and I'm certainly not upholding it as a model of good behaviour, but sometimes it's necessary.

Woman: Yeah, once I'm immersed in creating something, I usually maintain that state until I complete the work. And I don't even feel as if I am working. But if I look at the task ahead of me, all I tend to see is the effort involved!

Man: Right. And what about stuff you wrote ages back? Do you return to it for inspiration?

Woman: Well, I find I can't always recreate the mindset I had during its creation, because inevitably I've since broadened my perspective on it. I can see why I used the inspiration I did, but obviously experience changes you.

Man: Yes ... absolutely.

[pause]

tone

[The recording is repeated.]

[pause]

That's the end of Part One.

Now turn to Part Two.

[pause]

PART 2   *You'll hear a woman called Janine Rogers giving a talk about her work.*

For questions 7–14, complete the sentences with a word or short phrase.

You now have 45 seconds to look at Part Two.

[pause]

tone

Janine: Hello, everyone. My name is Janine Rogers, and I've got what many people would regard as a dream job – I'm a chocolate taster! My route into the job came after graduation. As a qualified chemist, I was looking to specialise as a lab technician, but when nothing came up, I considered retraining as a chef. Then I spotted a vacancy in the company I'm in now – and that's where my career started.

Everyone has a very specific professional title, mine being Product Developer. It doesn't cover everything I do, but it perfectly describes one aspect of the role.

My background has been a real asset to my work here. I'm currently creating the perfect fillings for our chocolates – at the moment it's caramel. But last month I had to come up with a way of introducing bubbles into the chocolate mixture. It may sound trivial, but it's what sells the chocolate! And I suspect only someone with my technical knowledge would've had the know-how to pull that off.

It may sound wonderful to work with chocolate all day, but it's not exactly a simple substance to work with – I'd even go so far as to call it problematic. That's because we're using a blend of fat as well as cocoa, which means the approaches we use, and the time we spend blending it can be crucial.

A lot of variables can affect how chocolate tastes – it doesn't naturally occur as the sweet-tasting confection we're all familiar with. Things like the climate of the region where the beans are grown have an effect, as does the technique used for drying them and the amount of sugar we put in the chocolate.

I spend about 20% of my time actually tasting chocolate. But of course, the end result is all the work of a team. For example, the marketing team will come up with a concept for a new range – and it's my job in Research and Development to bring that idea to life. Then we'll make samples and test them on consumers.

After that we'll speak to the engineers in manufacturing, and also the people in charge of packaging which, believe it or not, is an essential early stage. There's no point in creating something that can't be wrapped up and sold. Liquid chocolate is a good example – it's delicious, but difficult to preserve in that state for sale.

We also rely heavily on advice from our legal team about the claims we make for our chocolate in our advertising. And we need to be aware whether we're making something that's not suitable for vegetarians, say, but we haven't stated this in our labelling.

So what qualities are required in my job? Well, a curiosity about how things work and why, but above and beyond all else, you need initiative, and lots of it. There'll be times when no-one's giving you specific instructions and you need to get on by yourself. And of course, you need to love chocolate!

[pause]

Now you'll hear Part Two again.

tone

[The recording is repeated.]

[pause]

That's the end of Part Two.

Now turn to Part Three.

[pause]

PART 3   *You'll hear part of an interview with two sports psychologists called Shelia Forbes and Peter Maxton. For questions 15–20, choose the answer (A, B, C or D) which fits best according to what you hear.*

You now have 70 seconds to look at Part Three.

[pause]

tone

Interviewer: Today I'm with Peter Maxton and Sheila Forbes, both sports psychologists helping professional footballers prepare mentally for their performances. Welcome, both of you.

Peter; Sheila: Thank you.

Interviewer: So Sheila, how would you define your role?

Sheila: It can vary depending on the individual I'm working with, but basically, I equip players with techniques to improve their performance. Initially, though, I have to make sure they understand what I do and show them what they'll get out of it, so that they're properly on board from the outset. In my experience, players generally don't have tangible strategies to deal with the ups and downs that the game bombards them with, so I train them how to 'think' on the pitch – how to structure their thinking, be more confident themselves, and not be intimidated by the apparent confidence of others.

Interviewer: So how do you set about achieving your goals?

Sheila: Well, through a range of different approaches. I might set up a simulation of a performance, say, during which I'll be observing players for signs of repetitive patterns in behaviour and thought processes that can have a damaging effect on what happens on the pitch. Then I'll set about seeing where they're coming from, and begin the process of slowly breaking these patterns, using imagery or anxiety control. But players have to feel I'll respect confidentiality. After all, they're almost admitting to what might be interpreted by others as weaknesses in their mental approach, which in turn might raise questions about their suitability as a team member.

Interviewer: So what does a sports psychologist need to bring to the job?

Sheila: Well, during my career I've worked in a number of sports, such as boxing and horse riding. None of them are sports I've ever performed in, and in any case that's not demanded. What <u>is</u> needed though is that you understand the mental demands of those sports, and are able to adapt your work so that it can be integrated into the performance environment. But if you're not honest to your clients about what you realistically can and can't do, you won't progress very far.

Interviewer: Peter, would you agree with Sheila?

Peter: Well, my experience as a psychologist has been limited to football. But I'd add that you also have to be independent as you often have to make key decisions about an athlete on your own. But I'd certainly go along with Sheila's point about frankness. That's paramount, I'd say.

Interviewer: But you played sport as a student, didn't you Peter?

Peter: Well, I've never been a professional sportsperson, but I did play a lot of golf and tennis as a student, and was quite promising, although I don't think I took either of them terribly seriously. Then I hit what I can only describe as a stale patch and couldn't figure out why I was no longer up to standard. It eventually turned out that I'd been playing while suffering from an illness, a kind of fatigue syndrome. There wasn't the kind of monitoring you'd get nowadays that could have detected this earlier, and I was rather taken aback to discover there was no support when I switched back into playing again. That sparked my interest in the link between psychology and performance.

Interviewer: So Peter, is there anything you dislike about the job?

Peter: Well, it does get a bad press in some quarters, with people suggesting we're simply doing this for financial gain and realistically can't help top sports people up their game. But all we're doing is ensuring optimal conditions for athletes to achieve a consistently high level of performance. There's a constant shift in environments, of course, but personally I find that stimulating – and even within one club, you have a range of players and situations, and the techniques you learn are extremely transferable, as long as you're creative enough to do that.

Interviewer: So what do you both see as the future for sport psychology?

Sheila: Well, as an industry, it does have a developmental path for professionals coming into it, with young people with specialist skills coming through now. But there's still some PR work for us to do. We're still treated with a certain amount of suspicion by fans, simply because they don't understand what we do.

Interviewer: Peter?

Peter: I hope the use of psychology becomes more mainstream in both player development and coaching education. But, as Sheila said, there are still barriers to be broken down and psychology in sport should be put in perspective. It's part of the process of creating champions, which should be more widely publicised as a force for good.

[pause]

Now you'll hear Part Three again.

tone

[The recording is repeated.]

[pause]

That's the end of Part Three.

[pause]

PART 4 *Part Four consists of two tasks.*

You'll hear five short extracts in which students are talking about their universities.

Look at Task One. For questions 21–25, choose from the list (A–H) the reason each speaker gives for choosing their university.

Now look at Task Two. For questions 26–30, choose from the list (A–H) what each speaker found hardest at the start of their first year at university.

While you listen, you must complete both tasks.

You now have 45 seconds to look at Part Four.

[pause]

tone

Speaker One: My parents weren't happy when I told them I wanted to study law. The thing is I'm a keen athlete and so having a state-of-the-art track onsite to practise on after classes was crucial. They'd have preferred me to study in my city so I could've lived at home, which would've been much cheaper and easier of course. Anyway, I think I made the right choice. It didn't take long to start hanging out with some great people I met through lectures and my running. What was more of an issue was getting through all the stuff we were given to do. I had to be up all hours to begin with. I think I've finally cracked it now though.

[pause]

Speaker Two: Nothing prepares you fully for starting university life. I was away from home during the week with a whole new group of people who I would have to get to know. Strangely, though, what threw me most was figuring out where to do my assignments. After various unsuccessful attempts, I settled on a quiet spot in the student centre and then I could really focus at last. Choosing a university was straightforward actually. Since I'm studying history I thought a brand new campus wouldn't feel right. I wanted to gaze at ancient spires and towers on my way to lectures. That won hands down in the end against studying with one of my former classmates.

[pause]

Speaker Three: Selecting the right university was tricky. My dad would've liked me to study medicine close to home, but I also had to consider how the qualification I got would be valued in future. I mean, would the university command sufficient respect overseas, and that's what swung it for me. When I actually started, it took time to settle in. It was so different from school, where we all followed a fixed timetable term after term. My lectures are mostly after lunch, but I've got laboratory sessions at various times. Working all that out wasn't easy. Then I had to cook for myself too, though that broke up the hours of study a bit.

[pause]

Speaker Four: After school, I worked for my father for ten years and then decided to get a business qualification. I thought exchanging working life for one full of lectures and assignments would be demanding, which was true up to a point. I'd also thought getting my head round what the tutors were explaining would be straightforward, but that turned out to be a false hope. I'd taken time finding the right college. Partly because of my age, I followed lots of student blogs from various institutions to find one which offered some sort of mentoring service to help me settle in. That seemed vital. I was lucky that my first choice was surrounded by great mountains, but also easily-accessible from home – an added bonus!

[pause]

Speaker Five: I'd always wanted to study languages, but exactly which aspect, you know, linguistics, literature, drama and so on, well I kept changing my mind. It struck me what I needed was a university with lots of academic options, so I could experiment a bit. The one I picked also had a huge campus with loads of clubs and places to hang out, which was amazing. So I was never at a loss for something to occupy me on Saturdays. The downside of that massive campus was that everything was so spread out, and I had real difficulty trying to track the various teaching sites. I was forever apologising to tutors for creeping in way after their sessions had got going.

[pause]

Now you'll hear Part Four again.

tone

[The recording is repeated.]

[pause]

That's the end of Part Four.

There'll now be a pause of five minutes for you to copy your answers onto the separate answer sheet. Be sure to follow the numbering of all the questions. I'll remind you when there's one minute left, so that you're sure to finish in time.

[Teacher, pause the recording here for five minutes. Remind students that they have one minute left.]

That's the end of the test. Please stop now. Your supervisor will now collect all the question papers and answer sheets.

CAMBRIDGE ENGLISH
Language Assessment
Part of the University of Cambridge

Do not write in this box

SAMPLE

Candidate Name
If not already printed, write name
in CAPITALS and complete the
Candidate No. grid (in pencil).

Candidate Signature

Examination Title

Centre

Supervisor:
If the candidate is ABSENT or has WITHDRAWN shade here

Centre No.

Candidate No.

Examination Details

0	0	0	0
1	1	1	1
2	2	2	2
3	3	3	3
4	4	4	4
5	5	5	5
6	6	6	6
7	7	7	7
8	8	8	8
9	9	9	9

Candidate Answer Sheet 1

Instructions

Use a PENCIL (B or HB). Rub out any answer you wish to change using an eraser.

Part 1: Mark ONE letter for each question.

For example, if you think **B** is the right
answer to the question, mark your
answer sheet like this:

| 0 | A | B | C | D |

Parts 2, 3 and **4:** Write your answer clearly
in CAPITAL LETTERS.

For Parts 2 and 3 write one letter
in each box. For example:

| 0 | E X A M P L E |

Part 1

1	A	B	C	D
2	A	B	C	D
3	A	B	C	D
4	A	B	C	D
5	A	B	C	D
6	A	B	C	D
7	A	B	C	D
8	A	B	C	D

Part 2

Do not write
below here

9		9 1 0 u
10		10 1 0 u
11		11 1 0 u
12		12 1 0 u
13		13 1 0 u
14		14 1 0 u
15		15 1 0 u
16		16 1 0 u

Continues over ➡

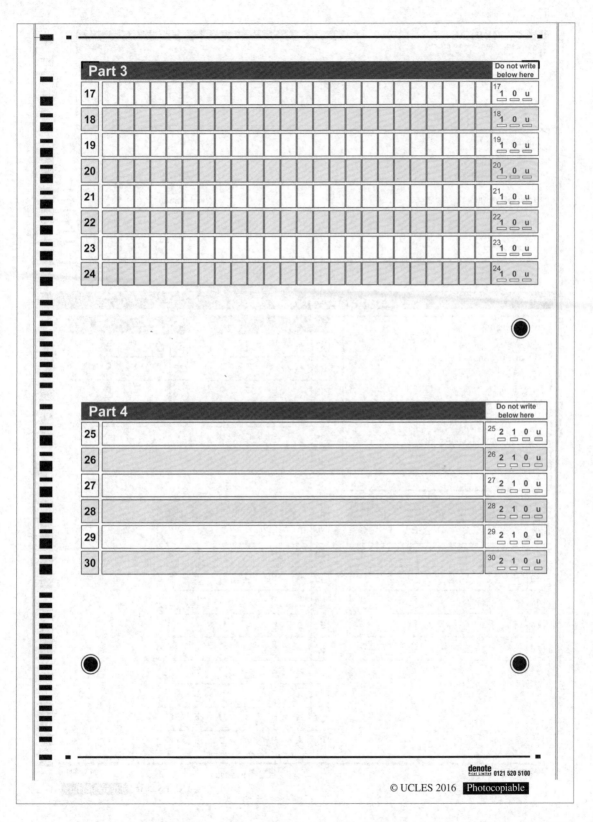

Part 3

		Do not write below here
17		17 1 0 u
18		18 1 0 u
19		19 1 0 u
20		20 1 0 u
21		21 1 0 u
22		22 1 0 u
23		23 1 0 u
24		24 1 0 u

Part 4

		Do not write below here
25		25 2 1 0 u
26		26 2 1 0 u
27		27 2 1 0 u
28		28 2 1 0 u
29		29 2 1 0 u
30		30 2 1 0 u

denote Print Limited 0121 520 5100

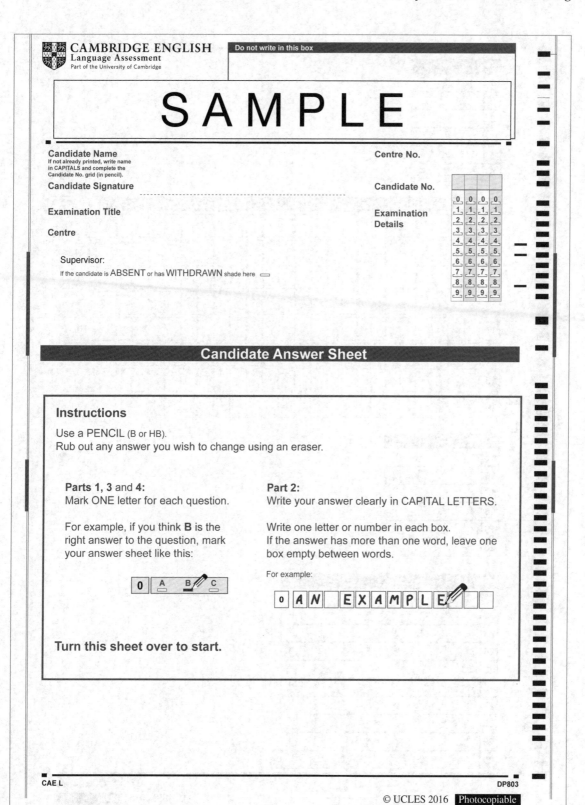

CAMBRIDGE ENGLISH
Language Assessment
Part of the University of Cambridge

Do not write in this box

SAMPLE

Candidate Name
If not already printed, write name
in CAPITALS and complete the
Candidate No. grid (in pencil).

Candidate Signature

Examination Title

Centre

Supervisor:
If the candidate is ABSENT or has WITHDRAWN shade here ▭

Centre No.

Candidate No.

Examination Details

Candidate Answer Sheet

Instructions

Use a PENCIL (B or HB).
Rub out any answer you wish to change using an eraser.

Parts 1, 3 and 4:
Mark ONE letter for each question.

For example, if you think **B** is the
right answer to the question, mark
your answer sheet like this:

Part 2:
Write your answer clearly in CAPITAL LETTERS.

Write one letter or number in each box.
If the answer has more than one word, leave one
box empty between words.

For example:

Turn this sheet over to start.

CAE L

DP803

© UCLES 2016 Photocopiable

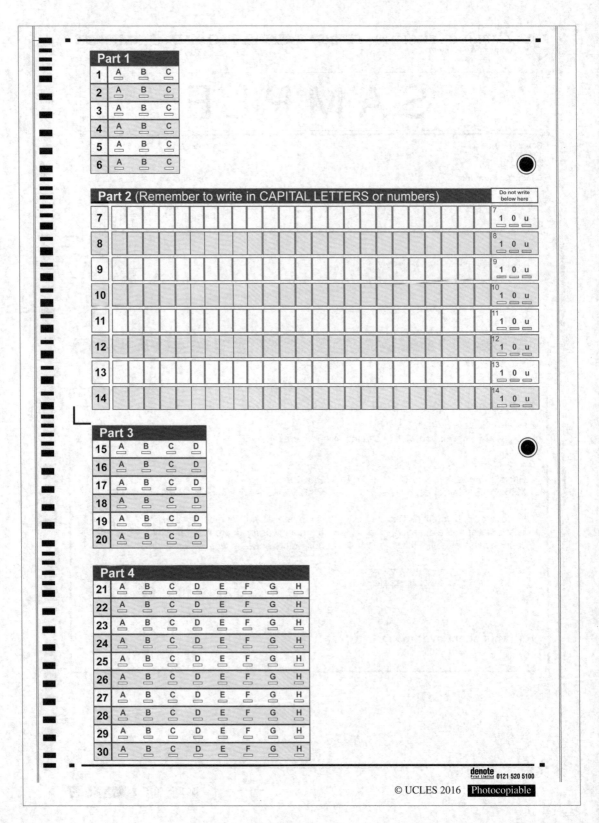

Thanks and acknowledgements

The authors and publishers acknowledge the following sources of copyright material and are grateful for the permissions granted. While every effort has been made, it has not always been possible to identify the sources of all the material used, or to trace all copyright holders. If any omissions are brought to our notice, we will be happy to include the appropriate acknowledgements on reprinting and in the next update to the digital edition, as applicable.

Text acknowledgements

Guardian News and Media Limited for the text on p. 10 adapted from 'Doodling should be encouraged in boring meetings claims psychologist' by Ian Sample, *The Guardian*, 27.02.2009. Copyright © Guardian News and Media Limited 2009; New Scientist for the text on p. 11 adapted from 'Super-rice defies triple whammy of stresses' by Andy Coughan, *New Scientist*, 28.02.2014. Copyright © 2014 Reed Business Information Ltd. All rights reserved. Distributed by Tribune Content Agency; Guardian News and Media Limited for the text on p. 14 adapted from 'Social media is the ideal way to get a job, but you can also ruin your chances' by Katie Morley, *The Guardian*, 09.04.2014. Copyright © Guardian News and Media Limited 2014; National Geographic Society for the text on pp. 18–19 adapted from 'Oman Climb-Impossible Rock' by Mark Synnott, *National Geographic Magazine*, January 2014. Used by permission of National Geographic Society; National Geographic Society for the text on p. 21 adapted from 'Mystery of risk' by Peter Gwin, *National Geographic Magazine*, June 2013. Used by permission of National Geographic Society; Women's Feature Service for the text on p. 30 adapted from 'Barefoot, female and a solar engineer' by Shruti Gupta, January 2003. Used by permission of Women's Feature Service; Telegraph Group Media Limited for the text on p. 32 adapted from 'Choose a Workplace You Love and You Will Never Have to Work A Day In Your Life', *The Telegraph*, 24.04.2012. Copyright © Telegraph Group Media Limited 2012; New Statesman Limited for the text on p. 36 adapted from 'The rest is noise' by Peter Wilby, *New Statesman Magazine*, 07.02.2014. Used by permission of New Statesman Limited; New Scientist for the text on pp. 40–41 adapted from 'City of Heat' by Chelsea Wald, *New Scientist*, 13.04.2013. Copyright © 2013 Reed Business Information Ltd. All rights reserved. Distributed by Tribune Content Agency; Kelsey Media Ltd for the text on p. 43 adapted from 'Why radical boredom could benefit you' by Matt Chittock, *Psychologies*, 15.04.2014. Reproduced by kind permission of Kelsey Media Ltd; Guardian News and Media Limited for the text on p.52 adapted from 'How a change of font could save $370m' by Jon Henley, *The Guardian*, 01.04.2014. Copyright © Guardian News and Media Limited 2014; Daily Mail for the text on p. 54 adapted from 'Up the creek with a paddle – It's the new celebrity fad but stand-up paddle-boarding is harder than it looks' by Lucy McDonald, *Daily Mail*, 03.09.2013. Copyright © Associated Newspapers Limited; Gulzaar Barn for the text on p. 58 adapted from 'Will Virgin staff really be allowed to take 'as much holiday as they want'?', Practical Ethics Blog, 25.09.2014. Reproduced with permission; New Scientist for the text on p. 60 adapted from 'How much can you trust your own memory?' by David Robson, *New Scientist*, 04.07.2012. Copyright © 2013 Reed Business Information Ltd. All rights reserved. Distributed by Tribune Content Agency; National Geographic Society for the text on pp. 62–63 adapted from 'The Smithsonian disassembles its dinosaurs' by Jane J. Lee, *National Geographic Magazine*, 31.07.2014. Used by permission of National Geographic Society; News Syndication for the text on p. 76 adapted from 'Power steps: why walking is the best exercise at any age' by Peta Bee, *The Times*, 23.08.2014. Copyright © News Syndication 2014; National Geographic Society for the text on p. 80 adapted from 'Our Vanishing Night' by Verlyn Klinkenborg, *National Geographic Magazine*, November 2008. Used by permission of National Geographic Society; Syon Geographical Ltd. for the text on pp. 84–85 adapted from 'A heated debate' by Daniel Allen, 01.02.2014. Copyright © 2014 Syon Geographical Ltd. Reproduced by kind permission of Paul Presley; Guardian News and Media Limited for the text on p. 87 adapted from 'Natural born linguists: what drives multi-language speakers?' by Martin Williams, *The Guardian*, 05.09.2013. Copyright © Guardian News and Media Limited 2013; News Syndication for the text and listening (Audio Script) on p. 122 adapted from 'Nicolas Jaar at the Roundhouse, NW1' by Ed Potton, *The Times*, 07.02.2012. Copyright © News Syndication 2012; Guardian News and Media Limited for the text and listening (Audio Script) on p. 123 adapted from 'Success in the workplace through sustainability' by

Visual materials for the Speaking test

- Why might the people have chosen to be in these isolated places?
- What problems might they face?

Visual materials for the Speaking test

- What skills might the people need to do this painting?
- How enjoyable might the activities be?

at school or college

choosing a career

What sort of help and support might people need from others in these different areas, and why?

in the working environment

in understanding technology

with financial issues

Visual materials for the Speaking test

- What might these people be celebrating?
- How long might they have prepared for these celebrations?

- Why might the people be checking this information?
- How useful might the information be?

- What sort of help and encouragement might the people be giving?
- How useful might this be?

- Why do you think the people are collecting these things?
- What satisfaction might they get from doing this?

Fashion style

Work and studies

How important is it to get advice when making decisions about these things?

Money matters

Travel and holiday opportunities

Free time activities / hobbies

- What can be annoying in these different situations?
- What might happen next?

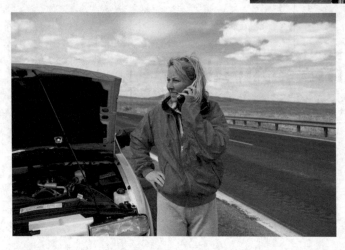

- Why might the people be looking at these things?
- How important is it for them to look at these things carefully?

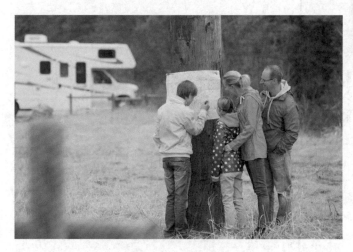

A sense of humour

Trust and respect for each other

How can these things affect the experience of working together in a team?

Team-building activities

Different salaries

Willingness to share ideas

Cambridge English

OFFICIAL EXAM
PREPARATION
MATERIALS

CAMBRIDGE.ORG/EXAMS

What do we do?

Together, Cambridge University Press and Cambridge English Language Assessment bring you official preparation materials for Cambridge English exams and IELTS.

What does *official* mean?

Our authors are experts in the exams they write for. In addition, all of our exam preparation is officially validated by the teams who produce the real exams.

Why else are our materials special?

Vocabulary is always 'on-level' as defined by the English Profile resource. Our materials are based on research from the Cambridge Learner Corpus to help students avoid common mistakes that exam candidates make.

Authentic examination papers: what do we mean?

PRETESTING

INVOLVING WRITING TEAMS AROUND THE WORLD

VALIDATION

PRACTICE PAPERS

SELECTION

LIVE EXAMS

Testbank

NOW ALSO AVAILABLE ONLINE IN Testbank

Practice makes perfect!

Discover more
Official Preparation Materials

Courses, self-study,
learner support